WITHDRAWN

THE CHURCH:
CHANGE OR DECAY

The Church: Change or Decay
Michael R. Tucker

TYNDALE HOUSE
PUBLISHERS, INC.
WHEATON, ILLINOIS

LIBRARY OF CONGRESS CATALOG CARD NUMBER 77-93750
ISBN 0-8423-0277-8, PAPER
COPYRIGHT © 1978 BY TYNDALE HOUSE PUBLISHERS, INC.
WHEATON, ILLINOIS 60187. ALL RIGHTS RESERVED.
FIRST PRINTING, MAY 1978
PRINTED IN THE UNITED STATES OF AMERICA

CONTENTS

Preface   7

Introduction   9

One   Provide Freedom for Change   23

Two   Plan Procedures for Change

Three   Propagate Unity to Encourage Change   77

Four   Organize Properly   105

Five   Purposely Compromise for Change   123

Six   Promote Big Goals   135

Seven   Practice Courage   151

Eight   Protect People   161

Nine   Preach Grace   171

Footnotes   191

PREFACE

The church.

How I love it!

How I hate it!

It fulfills my needs.

It frustrates me.

I shall always minister through the church.

I quit! God can use me in some other ministry.

For years I wrestled with my ambivalence toward God's people known as the church. I asked, "Why doesn't somebody do something?" Then I realized, "*I*'m somebody!" My life turned around when I awoke to the possibility that the church *can* change. And I can help lead in creating some of that change. Amazing!

Since my conversion to Christ, I have believed that the church belongs to God, and the gates of hell shall not prevail against it. But when I saw how the church was operating, I was impressed with God's patience toward his people. Surely there must be a better way to go about God's business than the ways I observed in most churches.

So I set about to minister in the church. Fortunately God dropped me into a setting where people were willing to grow in Christ and try some innovative changes. The changes were not instantaneous. Change always requires time. But within a few years a very traditional and spiritually dead church was alive and growing. Result: A model for others to follow.

Tyndale House graciously published the church's story in *The Church That Dared to Change*. I wrote that book to illustrate how God brought new life in one church—not to say that what happened in Colorado Springs was the *only* way. But ever since that publication in 1975, people have asked me, "How does one create change in an established church?" Again and again, weary pastors, anxious seminarians, and discouraged Christians in pews have pushed me against the wall. They want to know whether any set of rules will lead to change in the church. My honest answer has been, "I don't know."

So I set about to discover the answer. If church leaders follow certain principles, will change always take place? I observed, read, researched. I talked, listened, prayed. And I came to a conclusion. I now believe that orderly change will take place in any church that applies certain principles.

In fact, just before this book went to press, "orderly change" was effected in the church I serve. The board voted to change the name of the group (formerly Temple Baptist Church) to The Pulpit Rock Church.

This book is not for the rebel or the revolutionary. Nothing here is so avant-garde that it will appeal to only the most progressive Christians. This book is for the church leader, vocational or layman, who is tired of the way his church is functioning. It's for the Christian who wants to see important changes in his/her church. Here the interested Christian can find motivation to hang in there and produce change in his own assembly. Here you will find assurance that change can occur. And you will discover ideas and practical steps to use as you lead your church in ministering more creatively.

This book is not for the one who has already discarded the church. It's for the one who loves the church and sees it as essential in God's program. If you have been frustrated with the church, if you have wept for your church, if you want to create orderly change from within your church, read on.

INTRODUCTION

The president of a Christian school twisted his way down the narrow aisle of the airplane and dropped into his assigned seat in the coach-class section. In the seat next to him sat the president of the school from which he had graduated two decades earlier. During those twenty years so much water had rushed under the bridge that the bridge had collapsed between the two men. They were now in different Christian camps.

The former student saw this unusual circumstance as an opportunity to reconstruct the bridge. He warmly greeted the president and reintroduced himself. The older man offered a cool, formal smile when he recognized the other's name. But the former student grabbed his tools and started on that bridge.

"How are things at school?"

"Fine."

Not easily discouraged, he tried again. "Tell me, what are some of the changes since I left the campus so long ago?"

Dryly the president responded, "There have been *no* changes since then. We still hold the same truth and wave the same banner."

"Well," said the other, "I mean, I know you have built a beautiful new cafeteria. What other changes have taken place?"

"Absolutely none. The cafeteria's the only change!"

The bridge-builder put up his tools, eased his magazine up to his face, and sat in silence the rest of the trip.

"The old-fashioned gospel." "The old-time religion." "We haven't changed our direction one whit since our beginning." These phrases and statements represent some Christians' attitude about change. They see change as inherently evil. They perceive that God gets angry when he discovers change among his people or in his work. They have overlooked the simple truth that no progress occurs without change. Howard Snyder says:

God is a God of newness. On the one hand he is the Ancient of Days, "the Father of lights with whom there is no variation or shadow due to change" (James 1:17), and Jesus Christ is "the same yesterday and today and forever" (Hebrews 13:8). But this does not mean that God is static or stationary. The history of God's people in the Bible and the history of the Christian church show just the opposite. In every age the true biblical gospel is a message of newness and renewal.[1]

In 1865 a newspaper editor told his readers, "Well-informed people know that it is impossible to transmit the voice over wires and that, were it possible to do so, the thing would be of no practical value." Barely a decade later, the telephone erupted from Mr. Bell's laboratory and changed the world.

On the very day that the Wright brothers took wing, newspapers refused to report the event because their sober, solid, feet-on-the-ground editors simply could not bring themselves to believe it had happened. After all, a famous American astronomer, Simon Newcomb, had not long before assured the world that "No possible combination of known substances, known forms of machinery and known forms of force, can be united in a practical machine by which man shall fly long distances."[2]

As the 1970s give way to the 1980s, and beyond that to the year 2000, changes of all kinds will leave their imprint on U.S. society. Not only Americans, but other peoples will learn to adjust themselves to a new age that will operate in a framework of computerization, lasers, atomic energy, and satellite telecommunications now spreading over the globe. The result, many scholars believe, is likely to be a "hinge of history," opening up to an era in which people's attitudes, ways of life, and institutions may shift much as they did when the Industrial Revolution brought an expanding vista of space and time to the horse-drawn world of nearly two centuries ago. Science and technology, once the oracles for all problems, now are creating new problems as a result of their "solutions."

The poorest nations, with populations multiplying because of improved health conditions, already are burying their dead in famines. In America, the world's richest nation, our affluence and our education seem to be generating discontent, a scrambling of values, and social disarray. Everywhere, social reform and the heightening pressure for equality are placing governments under conflicting pressures of rival claims for attention. For sociologists, such conditions point the way to priorities that are likely to govern life and progress in years to come.

In Winnipeg, British educator Sir Eric Ashby told a symposium of scholars on "The Dilemmas of Modern Man":

We may expect immense pressures on every traditional value and belief as we adjust ourselves to constraints on population, on resources, on energy. The gyroscope of law which has kept society steady for generations is now wobbling under the influence of the urban guerrilla, the hijacker, the bomb planter. . . . The dilemma is that never before has so much self-discipline been needed from the public; and at the same time never before has the capacity to enforce discipline been so weak.

Pressures of congestion and shortages will continue to affect most Americans. Limits on industrial expansion and on single-family housing are foreseen. Apartment living will flourish in cities and suburbs. Public transit will grow sharply, and two-car families will become rare, predict the experts. Pollution will come under increasing control. Present trends suggest that, paradoxically, this control will occur more in urban than in rural areas; and more in inland waters than in oceans. Despite government limits on noise, the combined constant hum of background noise — from airplanes, cars, other machines, and voices will reach ever higher decibels as America gets more of everything.

The shift toward more leisure time shows no letup. Increasingly, Americans will be able to manipulate their working hours to mesh with personal interests—boating, concerts, athletic events, gardening, or family excursions. This trend is likely to accelerate the trend to more extended education beyond early years of life. As the twenty-first century moves closer, more people of all ages and economic groups are likely to be going to college full time or part time, for a few days or several years, for pleasure or for vocational or academic courses.

It's obvious that the world is changing. It always has and it always will. It should be just as obvious to Christians that they must change. The very simple truth is: life requires change. Therefore, the living church must be willing to change. Right here, however, we encounter tension. For evangelical Christians claim to work with a Bible full of absolutes. We talk shamelessly about the changeless Word of God.

The church as the body of Christ requires change. Ephesians 1:22,23 declares that the church is the body of Christ. All of the analogies in Ephesians and 1 Corinthians 12 point to the fact that the church is a living, growing organism. Any body must grow in order to be healthy. Growth requires change. Just as our bodies are continually changing, so the church must constantly be involved in change in order to be healthy.

Change is paradoxical. People do enjoy change. Even those who pretend that change is evil are constantly changing. Yet there is a natural resistance to change. The one who sees his destiny as that of changing a church, school, or Christian organization had better be prepared for joy and conflict, blessing and criticism, honor and hot water. A study of secretaries once revealed that the group tested responded with increased production to *every* change in working conditions (temperature, lighting, seating, etc.), including the changes that were for the worse!

"We must kneel and wash one another's feet in the church service," insists one group of Christians. Another demands that Christian women wear hats or scarves on their heads in the church meeting. One group believes it is wrong to play musical instruments in church. Some Christians immerse new converts in water, while others sprinkle a few drops of water on their heads. Some use wine for the communion service; others insist upon unfermented grape juice. The list goes on and on. Strangely, almost all Christian groups claim that their own practices (especially those that are unique to their particular group) arise from a careful study of the Bible. And usually each group is able to point to certain verses which seem to support their practices. What is the problem? Who's right and who's wrong?

Obviously the issue centers around the distinction between a biblical pattern and a biblical principle. You follow a pattern in specific detail. You develop your pattern according to over-arching principles which you may adapt according to your cultural context. The struggle for change rests here. The problem is that most of our current practices are not really founded upon biblical data but upon church tradition. Even those denominations and churches which say they eschew tradition are weighed down with forms, practices, and vocabulary which have developed through their own systems. Certainly not all of these traditions are bad. But you'll be hard pressed to find Bible verses on such common traditions as Sunday school, church buildings, financial budgets, missionary committees, nurseries, or hymnals. In the New Testament you find no examples of altar calls, ministers in robes, membership rolls, or tax-exempt status. Again, the point is not that any of these things are wrong, but that any attempt to change these things must be evaluated in terms of changing our traditions and not changing our belief in the Bible.

The society is changing and the church must change in order to do its job of reaching the society. In the United States a century ago there were two and one-half million people over age sixty-five. By the turn of the century an estimated thirty million citizens will be over sixty-five! The society has learned how to sustain millions of older people; now the church must learn how to serve them. How many churches do you know that have a minister of youth? Now how many do you know that have a minister to senior citizens?

Changes need not be like an avalanche. They can develop the way a snowball does. But they must develop. Peter Drucker says:

The need to slough off the outworn old to make possible the productive new is universal. It is reasonably certain that we would still have stagecoaches—nationalized, to be sure, heavily subsidized, and with a fantastic research program to "retrain the horse"—had there been ministries of transportation around 1825.[3]

The motto of some churches seems to be: There abideth faith, hope, and love; but the greatest of these is the status quo. Lyle Schaller puts it nicely:

Every organization, but especially non-profit organizations which do not have easy-to-read evaluations of the fulfillment of purpose, tend to move survival and institutional maintenance to the top of the priority list.[4]

How sadly true that the church often exists only for itself! Church leaders are frequently trapped into maintaining the inside rather than reaching the outside. No one really plans for this to happen. But some do not plan for it not to happen either. And that is the point. Unless we consciously plan change for the better, we will stay in the same ruts. The outside can always wait. In fact, the outside doesn't even know it needs us. So unless we go about change in earnest, we will continue to minister to ourselves and those few who recognize their need will have to come banging on our doors to ask for our help.

"Change the individuals and you will change the system" is only one way to create change. Change also works the other way. It is possible to change the system that will in turn change the individuals. For example, think how greatly the attitude of this nation has changed toward minority groups. A large part of that change came as a result of legislation. The system changed the people. Systems applied to groups are no less spiritual nor effective than systems applied to one individual at a time. When a church in the South voted to discontinue its practice of discriminating against Blacks, the attitudes of the individual members (even those who voted against the proposal) began to change. When an adult elective program started meeting needs in one church, the adults started attending Sunday school. The system changed the people. That is the heart of this book. We won't overlook *people* (see chapter 8), but neither will we overlook the need to change the system.

The wise person does not engage in change for its own sake. Hitting the nail on the head is a praiseworthy action, but only if the nail is needed and is in the right place. Some people seem to believe that *any* change is for the better. But remember that even death is a form of change. So is deterioration. Change can be so traumatic that death runs wild. One study of widows reveals that the death rate among widows the year following the death of their husbands is 700% higher than that of other women the same age.

The President of France, Gisard d'Estaing, publicly stated:

The world is unhappy. It is unhappy because it doesn't know where it is going and because it senses that if it knew, it would discover that it is heading for disaster. . . . The crisis the world knows today will be a long one. It is not a passing difficulty. It is actually the recognition of permanent change.

God's program is the church. The church is the body of Christ. The church is the *people*, not the building, the denomination, nor the organization. God's people are members of God's household, built upon the foundation of the apostles and prophets with Christ Jesus himself as the chief cornerstone (Ephesians 2:19,20). Statistics reveal that more Americans attend church in an average week than attend all professional baseball, basketball, and football games combined in the average year. All athletic events of all kinds, professional and amateur, draw about 5.5 million spectators per week, while churches draw 85 million worshipers in the same week.

Yet God has raised up many Christian groups outside the church. The character and progress of many para-church organizations give testimony that God is the founder of those groups. Christian schools, publishing houses, denominations, campus works, Bible study groups, and evangelistic associations are operating outside the church. We see no para-church movement in the New Testament. Yet few would dispute that God is behind those movements, without abandoning his work through his church.

The problem is that some Christians have abandoned the church in favor of para-church organizations. It is true that each Christian is a believer-priest, but that truth must stand in tension with other truth in the Bible. The New Testament offers no example of any Christian spinning off and doing his own thing. Can you imagine Paul's guiding a pagan Philippian to Christ and saying, "Now I'm going to meet with you each week to disciple you; just you and me, one on one," and leaving it there? Never! Paul got that new convert into a fellowship, a body, the church.

THE CHURCH: CHANGE OR DECAY 18

Consider what Alan R. Tippett writes in a book on church growth:

I submit, then, that the idea of a "churchless ministry" is unscriptural. Into what may the convert be incorporated if there is no fellowship? Our inheritance is a kingdom (Matthew 25:34) — a community concept.

If a "churchless ministry," in answer to the problems of the secular city, discards the church, it is also discarding Scripture, because Scripture commits believers to both the corporate group idea of the growing church and the idea of belonging.[5]

The church is a somewhat complex structure that recognizes the individuality of all its parts (1 Corinthians 12:12-26) and emphasizes the unity of the group (Ephesians 4:11-16). Every person in the church is important and needed. Even the abducter-digitee-minimee (the small muscle in the side of your hand that moves your little finger) Christian must function if the body is to do its work. The Bible speaks of the body as all Christians and as a local group. Each local church, regardless of size or impact, should consider itself the body of Christ. This is not so that the local church will be exclusive ("*we* are the body of Christ and others aren't because they don't practice our distinctives"), but so that each church, as well as each Christian, may recognize its importance.

Conversely, the church is a simple structure. When it operates as it should, its harmony and unity appeal to people on the outside. The inside overflows and draws in those who are watching. Bishop James L. Duncan, head of the Diocese of Southeast Florida, believes that the church does more for people than all the social-service agencies combined, and at half the cost. "Dollar for dollar," says the bishop, "no other institution that exists today gives greater service to humanity than does the church."

Linda was a new bride in a new city where her husband had obtained a good job. But first he had to go away for a month of training. During her husband's absence Linda tried to keep busy, but she really didn't have enough to do. She was lonely until she met an old boyfriend. There was good conversation, dinner, and then the pitch. Linda, a Christian, didn't want to be unfaithful to her husband, but because she was lonely and because she did enjoy the attention of the former boyfriend, she was afraid of her own emotions. One Sunday she attended a nearby church. The minister came to visit her the next week, and she told him about her problem. He advised that she get involved with God's program, the church. She did. Soon she was strong enough to tell the former boyfriend, who had become obnoxiously persistent, to leave her alone. Linda grew in Christ and became a vital part of that church, as did her husband, when he returned from his training.

The church has saved many people from ruining their own lives and the lives of those around them. Every minister can point sadly to people who drifted from the fellowship of God's people and are now paying the price in unhappiness.

The church must consistently remember that it is not here merely to serve itself. The purpose of the church is not to keep the organization smoothly operating. The church is not primarily to enjoy its own meetings. It is here to serve God and the world. As Ray Stedman says:

> The calling of the church is to declare in word and demonstrate in attitude and deed the character of Jesus Christ who lives within his people. We are to declare the reality of a life-changing encounter with a living Christ and to demonstrate that change by an unselfish, love-filled life. Until we have done that, nothing else we can do will be of any avail.[6]

God's people have not always had a difficult time defining their purpose. When God's people was Israel, they were a political entity as well as a spiritual group. As a nation Israel had wars to fight, peace to keep, an economy to oil, leaders to select and assassinate. They had lots to do. But the church is different. Now God's people must learn to operate in many different cultural settings and to relate God's message to each. And the church faces another difficult task besides. Says Harold Lindsell:

The church has the unpleasant task of witnessing to the world that the judgment of God is upon it. This appears to be a dismal and a gloomy business; it carries no message of optimism, only one of pessimism so far as the world itself is concerned. The world does not want to hear such a message, preferring to be told instead that things are as they always have been and that they are bound to improve.[7]

Two four-year-old twin girls arrived home after their first visit to Sunday school, talking enthusiastically about their experience. Mother took their papers and purses, but upon opening their purses, discovered that each still had every cent she had earlier given them. "Girls, why didn't you give your money to Jesus as I told you?" Without a moment's hesitation, they answered in unison, "He wasn't there."

Some people do look for Jesus in the church and cannot find him. To many the word *church* brings up visions of boredom. One cartoon shows a family in church with the little boy whispering to his dad: "You want to be playing golf; she wants to be home cooking dinner; I want to be playing football; what are we doing here?" In another cartoon a dad shows his little son a plaque on the church foyer wall. "This is in memory of those who died in the service," explained the father. "Which one," asks the boy, "the morning or the evening?"

Any honest Christian will admit that the church has failed in many areas. We do tend to create our own language and minister to ourselves. We have not done well at attracting the outside. The untaught must learn that the church calls the platform the chancel. Card tables are game tables. Benches are pews. The newcomer must learn when to keep quiet and when to say "uh, mmm" during prayer.

A nationwide survey reported in the September 13, 1976, issue of *U.S. News and World Report* that the public rates organized religion third in honesty, dependability, and integrity. Only banks and small businesses ranked higher. Rated lower than organized religion were the medical profession, educators, and the Supreme Court. (Politicians ranked last out of the field of twenty-six.) Yet when the same twenty-six institutions were ranked under the heading, "Ability to get things done," organized religion rated only thirteenth. Apparently people see the church as an honest and kindly entity that really doesn't seriously affect matters in the society.

The religion page of the *Southeast Missourian* for October 22, 1976, carried a story of a pastor who bragged, "I intend to have the largest church in this city. If winning people to Jesus Christ means using bribes and gimmicks to get people to church, then let me do it." So he offered a free turkey to everyone bringing fifteen people; every child riding the church bus would receive a goldfish.

Some have gone to such excesses to demonstrate their ability to get things done. Somehow, however, it appears that such programs are like the man from Colorado who went to Texas and bought a truckload of watermelons for a dollar each. In Colorado he sold all the melons for a dollar each. Then he counted his money and concluded, "I need a bigger truck!"

Part of the failure of the church is its belief that bigger is always better, and dust in the air represents forward movement. Findley Edge bites deeply when he expresses part of the failure of the church:

The word that I believe characterizes the major weakness in the life of the present church is superficial. Too many churchmen have only a superficial relationship with God, a superficial understanding of who God is and what he is about in the world, a superficial commitment to God, a superficial concern for the world, and a superficial involvement in the work God is doing in the world.[8]

The burden that gave birth to this book is that orderly change must be created from within the church. This work does not advocate an avalanche. The author is part of the church.

Outside pressures can never do what those of us on the inside can do. As you read the following pages, see yourself as one God can use to create change in the body of Christ. Your church can change. Take from this book what will benefit you now. Hold other material in the storage compartment of your mind for future use. Some parts obviously will not be helpful in your context at all.

It is not often that one has the privilege of hearing what others call him in the privacy of their homes. But a friend let it slip that around his house I am known as "Change-it Tucker." The family applied that title to me as a description of my approach to life and ministry. I consider the title a compliment.

One

PROVIDE FREEDOM
FOR CHANGE

25

Freedom in a System.

"What a wonderfully breezy day! Look at those two clouds race one another across the sky. I believe the little one is going to win. What a deep blue the sky is today! Oh, there goes a man's hat! I hope he catches it. And see those fellows on the baseball infield turn their backs as the gusts of wind kick dirt in their faces. I really enjoy the view from up here. Being a kite isn't such a bad life, most of the time. The only trouble — ugh, there it is! As I was saying, the only trouble is that string tied to my back and those rags on my feet. That clown on the other end of the string is Horace. He keeps me tied to him, and he lets out only a little string at a time. Why, without that guy and those rags, I could go where I wanted. I could fly higher than an airplane! I could be *free!*"

Well, anyone who knows anything about flying kites knows that our talking kite is all wrong. Without the string and rags, the kite would never fly at all. Without Horace giving gentle tugs, the kite would crash to the ground.

There are those who believe that freedom in the church should mean freedom to do whatever one wishes. But that kind of freedom leads to anarchy, not to flight.

Monsma, in an insightful book, writes:

In all this, one must keep in mind this paradox: To maximize true freedom it is necessary to limit personal freedom. To maximize true freedom is not to embrace absolute freedom. As noted earlier, if everyone could do whatever he pleased, no one would be free. Thus maximizing true freedom requires striking a balance between allowing free choice and curtailing free choice. This balance does not spontaneously arise in society, but must be sought by a self-conscious, painstaking process.[9]

Some Christians are like the kindergarten child who complained about the structured play period. After considerable griping and badgering, he succeeded in getting the teacher's consent. "All right, you may do whatever you wish." It must have given the teacher a heart full of satisfaction when the child returned and admitted, "I don't want to do what I want to do any more."

It is true that when we yield to any system we relinquish part of our personal freedom. But when we carefully choose our systems we gain much more than we lose. When a woman gets married she enters a system that drastically curtails her personal freedom. She no longer is available to accept dates from different men. She no longer can spend her money without checking with someone. She has a new schedule to keep and new responsibilities to uphold. But marriage brings a different kind of freedom. She becomes free to develop a deeper and more meaningful relationship than ever before. After marriage she has the freedom of an intimate union that is beautiful before God. This new system provides for a permanent relationship that is more satisfying than any benefits the old freedom could ever have provided.

That's what happens when you submit yourself to a relationship with the body of Christ. Although you can no longer "do your own thing" in an absolute way, you find plenty of freedom and support to enjoy happy and deep relationships in life and ministry.

Bob and Frank were long-standing friends who started attending the same church about the same time. At first they were overjoyed at the ministry of their new church. They were happy and helpful in every way. They pitched in and served at every opportunity. Since both men were highly gifted and experienced in the Christian life, the church gave them ample opportunities to minister. They moved rapidly into positions of leadership. Soon they were teaching adult classes. Their wives were also heavily involved in the church's ministry.

Then the leadership of the church noticed that Bob and Frank were offending people. They were insensitive toward other Christians. A closer investigation revealed that they were not cooperating with even the elementary rules of the system. They wouldn't keep accurate records for their classes. They would get substitute teachers without checking with anyone. They bypassed the committees in charge of their areas. They couldn't be bothered to cooperate with anyone about anything. When someone confronted them with these violations, they became defensive and argued that the system wasn't necessary. Yet it was the system that made it possible for them to teach and minister. It became quite obvious after a short while that both men wanted the system to provide them with people to allow them "to do their own thing," but they felt that they owed the system no allegiance whatever. After the break came, Bob and Frank tried to do their own thing apart from any system or church. They started their own church, but it failed miserably. The only ones who attended were their own families.

Professor Perry Landon of the University of Southern California points out that our country provided maximum personal freedom at a time when there was a wide measure of agreement and self-discipline concerning the limits within which freedom was to be exercised. As the consensus has deteriorated, the limits have been forgotten, and the exercise of freedom in various areas is pushing toward extremes that will unravel the fabric of society and ultimately force upon us a desperate choice between chaos and authoritarian control. Similarly, the church provides maximum personal freedom only when there is that heart commitment to the goals agreed upon by all. One part of the body cannot go in a different direction from the rest of the body. The body of Christ is not spastic! All members must cooperate with one another.

Others see the problem of freedom clearly and offer advice worth heeding. Secular prophet Alvin Toffler warns, "The problem is not whether man can survive regimentation and standardization. The problem is whether he can survive freedom."[10]

Martin Luther put it into the context of our faith: A Christian man is a free lord over all things and subject to no one; a Christian man is a subservient slave of all things and subject to every one. "For, dear brothers, you have been given freedom: not freedom to do wrong, but freedom to love and serve each other" (Galatians 5:13).

Writer Os Guinness sums it up: "Freedom with no form results in a reaction of form with no freedom."[11] The simple truth is that freedom operates best in a system. That is true for a society, a church, a kite.

Freedom to Allow Change.

Dean Brown arose at a faculty meeting in a large university during heated debate over including a course in the curriculum which the faculty opposed and the state legislature was pushing. "Fellow colleagues, the state legislature has always granted us complete academic freedom here," he said, "and if we don't do what they want us to do, they are going to take it away from us."

In a like manner, Pastor Jackson speaks often about a shared ministry. He encourages all members of the church to pursue, discover, and use their spiritual gifts. But the closer one gets to the inner circle, the more obvious it is: There is no freedom in his church. The freedom is in appearance only. Pastor Jackson holds veto power on all matters! That is discouraging to those who believe they have finally found a church that really wants to allow creativity and change. The sad part of the story is that it takes a while to learn the truth. Pulpit rhetoric can be misleading.

Freedom House reports that on planet Earth 1.3 billion people are citizens of "free" countries; 1.6 billion are citizens of countries "not free"; and 800 million are in "partly free" countries. Unfortunately no statistics tell how many churches practice freedom. But where there is desirable change there is freedom.

Lyle Schaller lists characteristics that usually can be found in a creative organization.[12] Part of the list can be applied to the church that provides freedom to change.

1. The primary orientation of the creative organization is to the contemporary social scene rather than to yesterday. Last week we took our children to a movie. At the refreshment counter we greeted a family from our church. "Naughty, naughty," jested the lady as she waved her index finger at us. I smiled on the outside but frowned on the inside. She really meant no harm, but I was mad. My children do not even know that the Christians of the last generation made movie attendance a test of spirituality. We are trying to raise our three to relate to their contemporaries and not

be burdened with holdover convictions which are no longer relevant. How long will Christians scratch where no one itches?

This principle answers a lot of silly questions about fads and fashions. "Love not the world and all that is in the world" refers to the values and standards of the world, not its recreation and fads. And besides, those who loudly denounce fellow Christians for relating to the contemporary worldly scene are themselves adhering to a worldly scene—the one of a generation ago.

2. The creative organization possesses a profound awareness that problems do exist. One of the refreshing breezes that blows across evangelicalism is the confession by recognized pastors and churches that they don't do all things right. No matter what church or pastor you have as a model, you will discover that that church and pastor are struggling just like all the rest of us. Oh yes, they may have had some success. They may be ahead of the pack. But they are aware of their problems. On the other hand, it is discouraging to see a church that won't even admit it has any problems. Being small and struggling is no disgrace, but failure to admit problems is. Some churches have no freedom to change because they've made no admission of need. And how could a fundamental, Bible-believing, soul-winning, premillennial, pre-tribulational, missionary-minded church ever have any problems?

In some churches all problems are buried in clichés such as: "All our problems are solved when we preach the Word, win souls, and send out missionaries." But the free church, like the free individual, can say, "We face a problem and we don't have an answer now." A few years ago at a conference I admitted my ignorance to a question asked in the seminar I conducted. I got such great response to that admission that ever since then I've felt wonderful freedom in question-and-answer sessions. (In fact, I almost overreacted and worked at saying "I don't know" at least once in every feedback session I conducted after my Sunday morning messages.)

3. Throughout the creative organization the primary focus is on people and people's needs. An entire chapter is devoted later

to this important concept (chapter eight). But let it be known now that there is great freedom in realizing that only God, his Word, and his created intelligent beings shall last forever. All else is temporary, and that includes the organization of the church. Where there is an option, always choose people over organization.

4. Within the creative organization the emphasis is on problem solving rather than on institutional maintenance or on keeping the operation running smoothly. Nothing kills a church's atmosphere of freedom to change more rapidly than the realization that this church really just wants to keep the same tired old programs and people in power. In some churches, when people with vision want to place a vital new emphasis on missions, they are burdened with the old machinery of its long-encrusted missionary group. Missions can't get to the people unless that group is involved. And too often that group resists all fresh approaches.

The truly free church lets people know that we take a fresh look at *all* parts of the organization in order to solve problems. If there is dissatisfaction with the music, maybe we need to scuttle the choir and create some ensembles. We discovered that the people weren't less spiritual because they failed to show up for the midweek Bible study. The facts were revealed in a survey: 87% of the adults were already in another weekday Bible study! The way to solve our problem of sagging attendance at the midweek Bible study was to cancel it. In this instance we didn't oil the machinery, we dismantled it.

When there was a need for more worship services, we faced another problem. Three morning services meant we were in a box and couldn't touch the machinery. We weren't afraid to; we just couldn't see how to do it. So we left the machinery intact that time and created a Saturday night service that operated for one and one-half hours, thus providing one more worship time which some could choose.

5. Leaders in the creative organization are clearly aware of the importance, relevance, and availability of knowledge from a vari-

ety of disciplines that they can apply in fulfilling their organization's purpose and achieving its goals.

Before I started my present ministry, I told the church that I would want to start a Christian school if I accepted the pastorate in Colorado Springs. There was not a Christian elementary or secondary school in the entire area. The people agreed. After I arrived, however, it became evident to me that starting a school is no small task. As we prayed about the matter, the Lord brought several other Christian men across my path. The men were from different churches, but all were interested in Christian education. Several had tried to start a school previously but could not generate sufficient interest from the Christian community. We met and talked and prayed for months. Then a nondenominational school was born. The new venture started with all thirteen grades. It enjoyed the immediate support of the Christian public, and has continued to prosper. Our church property has housed the school through these years, although we have also used other facilities from time to time. By cooperating with others, we were able to do what we could not have accomplished on our own.

In a recent year 1,200,000 American babies were drowned in salt water or pulled apart by suction, according to the National Right-to-Life Organization. These killings were called "the mother's right," and are listed as legal abortions. The high figure represents two killings (is murder too strong a word?) per minute!

We believe abortion is morally wrong. But what can one church do to fight this evil? One approach for us has been to encourage people to attend and support pro-life groups. We also have given free office space and janitorial service to a pro-life group. This approach has not detracted from our own ministry but has allowed us additional ministry through another group.

At the present time, our church officially endorses four Christian camps in our area. Currently we do not intend to go into the camping business ourselves. The four camps (and others that we cooperate with) are doing a fine job. A few years ago we were able to get several college campus workers to come to our city and begin a ministry in cooperation with our church. We helped support those people, but we did not bear the full burden of their support. At the height of that ministry, five full-time workers were relating college students to our church, yet none were actually on our church staff.

We are now in the process of conducting a feasibility study for a Christian radio station in our city. Although our city has 200,000 people, no Christian radio programming originates here at the time of this writing. Those doing the study are contacting other Christian groups and churches to discover whether anyone else is working in this area and whether others would like to cooperate with us. The same kind of study is now in progress to discover the activity in relation to opening a Christian counseling clinic.

Since we opened the doors of the Christian school in 1971, about six more such schools have started. Some of those have already folded. Not one of their leaders came to us and talked! We approached several of them and asked if we could work together, but not one was interested. Frankly, it is sad to see Christians "invent the wheel" over and over again. How long will we keep reduplicating efforts in order to hang onto a couple of our picky distinctives? There is freedom in going outside your own group and working with other organizations that can serve you, cooperate with you, and help you meet your goals for your own group and for the community. Why don't churches learn to cooperate with social service agencies in their own community? Certainly it is understood that secular groups won't present the gospel. But we can do that while the community groups take care of the physical and emotional needs of those in pain.

6. The creative organization maintains a continuing effort to monitor the pace of change that can be accommodated before the benefits of change are outweighed by the cost of disruption. One of my first experiences in creating change in the church occurred fifteen years ago when I was a minister of education in a church in California. I suggested that our traditional vacation Bible school for children be held in the afternoon rather than the morning. I was almost laughed out of the committee. The next year I tried

again, and met with a similar reaction. I never did get that change. But the year after I left, the church tried it and kept doing it for many years. To push for that change while I was there would have been so disruptive that the effect of the change would have been neutralized.

For the first two years in my present pastorate, I issued a public altar call every Sunday morning. The church was in that tradition. To depart from it too soon would have been disruptive. *Now* if I were to issue such a call, I would have to spend five minutes explaining what I was doing. In fact, to issue such a plea now would be quite disruptive!

God's timing is an important factor in determining God's will. In Acts 15, the Council at Jerusalem declared that Gentiles don't have to be circumcised in order to be part of the community of faith. Paul's side won. But in the very next chapter we read that Paul circumcised Timothy. He applied this principle of timing according to people's readiness.

When I first suggested to our church board that we allow fathers to baptize their own children, I met skepticism and resistance. But a patient search of the Scriptures led to the practice in our church in a short while without any disruption whatever. The truly free innovator doesn't allow change to create disunity. The whole point of this book is that orderly change must be created from within the church.

7. The creative organization uses a built-in self-evaluation process which is designed to test its present operation against its definition of purpose. This principle helped us decide to change the name of our church. We asked, "What are we trying to do?" Then we queried, "Does our name help or hinder?" There was little discussion about it: our name was hindering our purpose. (We aren't saying that our name would hinder another church in another context. But in our context, the name hurt us.) Again, there is freedom in asking hard questions about every part of the church. Why do we sing (or not sing) the doxology; repeat the Apostles' Creed; center the Sunday service around the preached Word; have special music; purchase an organ instead of fifty

banjos; group children in the Sunday school according to chronological age rather than spiritual maturity; encourage or discourage emotionalism in the worship service; have or not have a church roll; elect or appoint church officers? The list must include every part of the ministry, and especially our distinctives and sacred cows!

This is part of leadership. Leaders should gather and systematically evaluate the whole church. There may be very few things you will want to change. But you won't know that until you evaluate.

8. Within the creative organization, a goal frequently may change during the effort to reach it. An inner-city church decided to build a new educational wing to better accommodate the people who were attending. After the church had its plans drawn and its funding started, a buyer offered the church a large sum of money for its property. A shopping center was being proposed for their corner. They sold and moved. They had freedom to make that choice because they realized that their goals may change for the better before they ever accomplish them. The flexible and free church allows new data to influence its decisions and goals.

The goals of our Christian school were altered during the early 1970s when an economic crunch hit our city. Enrollment dropped. We had to cut back goals for new athletic programs and additional faculty and equipment. Often outside forces such as economic factors, weather, politics, and the general atmosphere of the community force a church to change its goals. The churches in Indonesia certainly changed their goals in the 1960s after the failure of a communist coup. New believers stormed their churches, and the churches had to alter virtually all their plans to accommodate the revival.

Internal factors also may indicate that goals should be altered. Personnel factors influence goals. We enjoy having a graded choir program in the church for our children. But several times we have had to put their projected activities on the shelf until Christians with the necessary gifts and burdens presented themselves to lead that ministry. Internal priorities are also a consideration. A church can't do all the things it would like to do all at once.

9. The financial administration of the creative organization places the primary emphasis on expenditures, costs, output, and program, rather than on receipts, revenues, and input. "Doesn't this church need any money? You never mention it around here." The Christian businessman who asked that question paid us a great, great compliment. Sure, we need money (this year's budget is over $300,000 and we are building a $1,250,000 building!). But this principle teaches us the freedom we can experience in not hustling money from God's people. When people are helped through a ministry, they usually have a burden to support that ministry. When people see that money is spent wisely, they freely support the ministry. Do you ever get weary of seeing figures of last week's offering as compared to the budget? Do you ever wonder if those figures appear only when the offering is less than the budget? If suddenly the offerings greatly exceeded the budget, would those figures be snatched from publication for fear that people would quit giving? Of all people, God's people should not be harangued about giving. Motivation should come through the Word and positive steps which illustrate, "Here is how the money in this organization is spent, and here is what it accomplishes."

10. The leadership of the creative organization attempts to maximize the staff's problem-solving capability rather than simply control the staff's time and compensation. Some church boards view their role as keeping the pastor(s) in line. They seem to cherish an unwritten rule which declares that a balance will be maintained in this church if the board shoots down about half of the pastor's ideas.

Surely a portion of the problem is that pastors come and go, but the core lay leadership of the church plans to stay until death. No wonder church leaders are frightened by creative innovation. The last pastor tried some of the same tricks. And when they failed, he left for another ministry. Meanwhile, the church leaders were left with the invoices and mess to clean up. It's little wonder they are now skeptical about new ideas. I believe a commitment to a long-term ministry by a pastor helps dilute some of those fears. This allows freedom of exchange without the fear that if the pastor gets mad or doesn't get his way, he will leave.

Churches are finally emerging from an era when pastors were paid in chickens and ego strokes. Church staff salaries are climbing to decent levels. The old adage that some church boards prayed, "Lord, you keep our pastor humble, and we will keep him poor" was no joke! But the wise church board gives freedom to those who lead full time. They compensate adequately so that the pastor has personal freedom also, and so his prayer time isn't spent praying for money to feed his family but for other people and the life of the church.

Furthermore, church leaders need to allow the church staff the freedom to expand their ministries well beyond the walls of one particular church. It is narrow thinking on the part of some churches to restrict their pastor's time to meeting their own needs. They are, in fact, cutting their own throats by controlling their leader's ministry in such a manner. A friend of mine was appointed Chaplain of the Senate in his state. Not one person in the congregation came and said, "We are proud of you. We support you in prayer. What an opportunity to influence our state leaders for Christ." Instead there was the grumpy comment, "I suppose this will mean you won't be available for us much anymore." Surely a balance must be maintained, but some ministry of a pastor away from his flock will enhance his ministry *to* his flock.

When George Romney left his government post as Secretary of HEW, someone asked him what he had learned. "I would say that the principal lesson I have learned is that you don't get basic social reform in this country without a crisis," Romney replied. He went on to explain that the chief hindrance to his programs was not a lack of money, but the lack of a constituency for change. Romney was clearly a defeated and discouraged man because he saw no freedom to believe that change could take place.

Many Christians live in the same defeated attitude. Some drop out of church. Others stay but really don't expect much. They are satisfied if the pastor isn't too boring on Sunday and if the church meets its annual budget. Meanwhile, leaders grumble about the lack of commitment and the materialism of the people. But Robert Townsend pounces on us with his words:

Probably whenever Sitting Bull, Geronimo, and the other chiefs powwowed, the first topic of conversation was the shortage of Indians. Certainly today, no meeting of the high and the mighty is complete until someone polishes the conventional wisdom: "Our big trouble today is getting enough good people."
This is crystal-clear nonsense. Your people aren't lazy and incompetent. They just look that way. They're beaten by all the overlapping and interlocking policies, rules, and systems encrusting your company.
Stop running down your people. It's your fault they're rusty from underwork. Start tearing down the system where it has defeated and imprisoned them. They'll come to life fast enough. Be the Simon Bolivar of your industry. Ole![13]

Freedom to Fail.
If there is reincarnation (and I know there isn't), I would like to be a pastor again the next time around. I'm learning so much on this trip that, by the time I'm an old man and ready to die, I should know how to be a pastor in today's world. In each of the classrooms in our educational building is a grim reminder of one of my failures. In a prominent place there is a piece of special paneling that was put there to replace a standard chalkboard. What a mistake! The idea was mine, and it was really a blooper. One of our board members insisted that the church purchase a button-making machine so that everyone would have a permanent nametag. So far: a failure. Last year's junior choir was a disaster. We bought the wrong kind of typewriter and wasted a bundle of money. Our first printing press never really worked well at all. Everyone who tried to operate it almost lost his sanctification. More than a few times I've almost blown a major decision because I didn't present it properly. A couple of times I've had to return to an audience and explain a point of a previous sermon because a misunderstanding was causing offense. Once we hired

a schoolteacher at the Christian school who had to be removed within one month of opening day. A public schoolteacher with twenty years of experience took on a children's church group as a ministry. She was torpedoed in three weeks and quit. On more than a few occasions we have put shelves in the wrong places and knocked unnecessary holes in walls. We put off for a year a decision to install another bathroom near the nursery because of the cost. The actual cost was less than half what we anticipated. We have made mistakes hiring janitors and letting musical groups minister at the church. We have been embarrassed by speakers and singers.

After a paragraph like that, I feel defensive and must say that we really aren't stumbling idiots. We do some things right. But we do lots of things wrong too. We make many mistakes. And we will continue to do so because we realize that progress involves risk, and risk produces errors. The errors are worth the freedom to fail.

In Pastor Hy N. Mighty's church he is respected on *every* issue. He has the last word on the new budget, the missionary support, and the broken toilet. He runs the show on which Sunday school curriculum to buy and who gets on the nominating committee. And, since he is a one-man show, no one dares to challenge him. That poor pastor may think he is free to run the church. In reality he is a slave. He can't afford to make errors. And when he does miscue, he must make an elaborate cover-up.

People need to know that they can fail and still be accepted. One way to accomplish this is to establish a system of assistants or helpers. Such a system provides for an individual to observe and help for a while without taking on the full responsibility. This practice also allows the person to make a sounder decision about whether that particular post is the one where he/she should be serving. Almost any ministry in the church could use an assistant. We even have this system extended to our official board of the church.

The freedom to fail must be extended beyond ministry and

into life. When a brother or sister falls into sin, there should be a loving body of believers ready to help that Christian back onto his/her feet. We do this with some sins, but too often we are selective. Usually we are willing to help someone on drugs. Alcohol isn't quite so acceptable. If there is a former Mafia member or big-time crook, we put him on the platform when he gets his life right with God. We allow him the freedom to fail and turn back to God. But in some churches if a person gets divorced, it's all over. The divorced person isn't allowed a place of ministry. Another unpardonable sin is an attack on the power structure (see chapter two). Even when the attacker admits his error, he is held at arm's length. That's because we fail to distinguish between disagreement and disunity (see chapter three).

On Sunday, March 27, 1977, the worst airplane disaster in history occurred when two 747s collided on the ground on the Canary Islands. Five hundred eighty people died. Only sixty-six survived. All of the survivors were Americans, and fifty-one of those were rushed to a military hospital in San Antonio, Texas, for treatment of burns. Investigation revealed that the pilot of the Dutch airliner misunderstood his directions from the tower. He thought he was cleared for take-off when he was actually on standby. Racing his 747 down the fog-covered runway, he rammed a Pan-American 747 about midway down the stretch. What a tragic mistake! But if every commercial pilot lives in fear that he will be guilty of the same failure, we will all be riding trains and buses. If pastors don't quit worrying about their jobs and lose their fear of failure, they will never progress. If Christians don't put aside their fear of failing God or the church (or the pastor?) and take some chances, we aren't going to see progress in the church. Says Albert Sullivan:

The right to fail is of the essence of creativity (just as the prevention of failure is of the essence of conservatism). The creative act must be uninhibited and marked by supreme confidence. There can be no fear of failure — nothing inhibits so fiercely, or shrinks a vision so drastically, or pulls a dream to earth so swiftly, as fear of failure.[14]

Dr. Robert Schuller, pastor of the Garden Grove Community Church in southern California, says he was cured of his fear of failure by the slogan, "I'd rather attempt to do something great and fail than attempt to do nothing and succeed."

Freedom to Bury the Dead.

In a book called *The Effective Executive*, Peter Drucker says;

The first rule for the concentration of executive efforts is to slough off the past that has ceased to be productive. Effective executives periodically review their work programs—and those of their associates—and ask: "If we did not already do this, would we go into it now?" And unless the answer is an unconditional "Yes," they drop the activity or curtail it sharply. At the least, they make sure that no more resources are being invested in the no-longer-productive past. And those first-class resources, especially those scarce resources of human strength which are engaged in these tasks of yesterday, are immediately pulled out and put to work on the opportunities of tomorrow.[15]

Perhaps it would help if we formed one more committee in our churches. The new committee would be responsible for burying the dead. For every new program, this committee would be charged with burying at least one other program (preferably two for one for a while). We need the freedom to discontinue the men's fellowship meetings rather than make men feel guilty because they aren't supporting the meetings. The women's Bible study worked well for a time, but now there is not much interest. Bury it! One church enjoyed getting missionary prayer requests in the bulletin each week. But now few people notice the requests or pray for the missionary. Discontinue the practice! There was a time when a certain church looked forward to the quarterly potluck suppers, but recently people don't seem interested. Maybe they don't enjoy fellowship with other Christians? Ridiculous! It's just that the method needs to be changed. Publicly introducing the new members and giving them "the right hand of fellowship" meets with little enthusiasm. Stop doing it!

Singing "Happy Birthday" each week in the Primary Department is a drag. Recognize the birthday people in a different way—or not at all.

Usually we do not have trouble getting rid of the total failures. The problem is with yesterday's successes. It worked so well for a time that we keep pumping air into the lungs of a dead horse, hoping it will be resurrected to former glory. But that doesn't often happen. It wouldn't be so bad, keeping these dead horses around, except that they deprive the important and alive ministries of our time, energy, and money. The women who regularly meet and roll bandages for missionaries could spend that time praying or visiting those in need. If the tracts aren't being used, remove the rack and replace it with a rack of Christian books.

On one of my first journeys to preach, I spoke in a small church in a nearby city. The head deacon told me before the service that when I asked the ushers to come and receive the offering, I should read the poem he handed me. It was a nice poem, and I asked why this poem on this Sunday. "Oh," he explained, "we read this poem *every* Sunday before the offering." "*Every* Sunday—the *same* poem?" "Every Sunday—the same poem," he emphasized. Well, I did as I was told. But at the evening service I forgot to receive the offering at all. (I've always wondered if that omission was an overreaction to the poem in the morning.) Although there weren't more than twelve or fifteen people present that evening, all of whom were there in the morning, I really thought those deacons were going to lynch me after the service. Never had anyone forgotten to receive an offering in that church! Frankly, I wouldn't be surprised if that church is still about the same size and still reading that same poem before the offering each Sunday morning.

One who wishes to create orderly change from within the church must begin with freedom. There must be a structure and attitude that encourage innovation. No one person should bottleneck the progress. If one person has veto power over all matters, there is not sufficient freedom. Yet if you don't have a certain amount of cooperation with the system you'll have chaos. The church that wants to change needs freedom to fail and freedom to bury the dead.

Two
PLAN PROCEDURES
FOR CHANGE

Recognize the Current Situation.

"Sally, give up your Messiah complex." I spoke these words in love to a member of our church staff. Sally was working herself into the ground. She was doing several jobs at once, though being paid only as a part-time business manager for the church. In addition, she had assumed responsibilities for oversight of the library and the audio-visual room. Her natural bent for orderliness pushed her into doing many housekeeping and maintenance chores that could have been done by someone else. Often she took personal interest in helping the janitorial staff. But now she was frustrated and discouraged.

"What is a Messiah complex?" she asked me. I explained that most of us in the helping professions have the sincere desire to assist people. Those of us who are Christians even connect this desire with our love for the Lord. We truly do want to serve people and honor God. But what often happens is that we believe that, given enough time, we can solve any problem. We believe that with sufficient opportunity we can work long enough and love big enough to get to the source and solution of any problem that confronts us. That is what I call a Messiah complex. Somewhere in life all of us must realize that there are certain problems we cannot solve. There are relationships we cannot heal. There are circumstances we cannot master. A wise leader will relinquish his Messiah complex and admit there are things he cannot do. Even in the church. You can pray and you can cry and you can hurt, but frequently that is all you can do. Besides, the person who gets 100 percent of his job done just does not have enough to do.

The lecture to Sally helped her. In a few days she had given up some of her responsibilities, and life was beautiful again. The reason I was able to deliver that lecture was that someone had delivered it to me years before. My first job around a church began when I approached my own pastor. I knew that his secretary had just quit and he was looking for a replacement. I volunteered for the job. At first he laughed at the suggestion, but then he recognized that I was serious. "You really want to work as a church secretary?" he asked. "Yes, I do." So I convinced him that I had the necessary skills to do the job.

The new relationship was a happy one. One problem, however, was that my workaholic tendencies began to show themselves. I was supposed to work only twenty hours a week, but I actually worked twice that amount of time. One day the pastor told me to quit and go home. He informed me that I could never get all the work done around the church. If I worked forty or sixty or eighty hours, there would still be more to do. So he told me to give up my Messiah complex.

Part of giving up your Messiah complex is to learn to work smarter rather than longer. Most leaders recognize that no meaningful and lasting change can take place without planning. Often the one working long hours is the one who does not plan well. The first step in planning is to recognize the current situation. Ask the question, "Just where are we in this organization?"

Alec MacKenzie, in *The Time Trap*,[16] gives some good illustrations. An insurance company that had never segregated its sales accounts by relative size decided this would be a good idea. It discovered that less than 10 percent of its accounts represented nearly 90 percent of its total sales volume. Yet, its overall efforts in selling and servicing accounts had never been targeted on this small but vitally important group. A radical policy change resulted in significant gains in sales and profits for the ensuing year, directly attributable to this approach.

Auren Uris tells how the president of a clock factory eliminated one-third of the company's models when he found they added up to only 4 percent of the company's sales volume. Within six months the firm was doing a larger and more profitable volume.

At our church we have discovered that surveys help us recognize where we are. In our surveys, which we conduct at least once each year, we ask where people need help. This allows us to plan our preaching and teaching better throughout the entire church program.

If people do not want help with family relationships, then we should know that. One survey revealed that people needed help in money management. Two of our men, one a teacher of economics and the other the director of stewardship for a Christian organization, studied for several months and put together a course as one of our adult electives. The size of the class had to be limited because the room would hold only 140 people. Many more wanted that course. On several occasions teachers in our church have published books which developed, in part at least, from the courses they taught at the church. The need for these courses surfaced through surveys. Once we even trained a group of people who went into every member's home to work through an extensive survey with each individual.

Surveys also help us to know why people attend our church, where we are making mistakes, and to which areas we need to give more attention. The surveys also bluntly demonstrate what is already dead and needs to be buried.

Our latest survey was anonymous. It provided excellent information about who we are. Already we had recognized that the congregation was a highly educated group, but we were amazed to learn that 71 percent of those taking the survey had a college degree and 21 percent had advanced degrees. The survey included everyone over thirteen years of age.

This survey gave us a good knowledge of the income level of the congregation. It was through this same survey that we learned that 87 percent of our people were involved in a weekday Bible study. And through a similar survey we learned that 95 percent of the people were in favor of changing the church's name.

People who have read the preface to *The Church That Dared to Change* (Tyndale House Publishers, 1975) often ask why I walked into such a sad situation. The church had recently dismissed its pastor. Bitterness remained after a vicious battle. Many people left. When the pulpit committee presented a candidate for the available pastorate, the congregation's vote was a majority to call him, but less than the three-fourths required to hire a pastor. Again there was in-fighting. More members left. The rejected candidate started his own church in the city and took about one-third of the members with him. The church was going under for the third time. The leaders were bruised and discouraged. Privately they agreed to shut the doors, sell the property, and disperse any remaining funds to missionaries. But through all of these problems some could see the potential for change at this church. The current situation was bleak, but the people were willing to make an effort. That made the difference.

In recognizing the current situation, leaders must learn to tackle problems according to priorities. Some of the changes that the rejected candidate wanted to institute in his first week have come five or seven years later. Maybe changing the church name is not as important as training church leaders. Organizing the Sunday school may take priority over organizing home Bible studies. At first, developing relationships with the power structure may be more important than visiting new people.

"That's a good idea. Let's do it. All those in favor raise your right hand. Good, that's settled. Pastor, would you take care of that for the committee? Of course none of *us* can, since we work or have children to care for." That approach is all too typical in most churches. The committee or board votes and the pastor is supposed to do the leg work. The effective leader who wants to create orderly change must learn to pronounce the word *no*. He should learn to say it gracefully, but in plain English. It isn't easy to say no and wonder if people will fire you. But unless leaders say the word, they will never get to the important matters of ministry in the church. One can't even observe and evaluate unless he has time to see what is really happening.

I have mentioned that we are currently involved in constructing a building which is costing 1.25 million dollars. Yet I probably have spent less than an hour with the building committee. The committee is chaired and operated by very capable people of the church. There have been times when I could have gotten involved, and frankly I would greatly enjoy that kind of involvement. Yet I have had to learn to kindly refuse further involvement in the building project. Likewise I cannot accept all counseling cases. Sometimes I must decline social engagements. I believe that every Pioneer Girls group and every Boys Brigade section is vitally important; yet I must recognize that I can visit those groups only occasionally. Learning to say no is no easy task, but the wise leader will learn to say it.

Define Underlying Problems.

Mrs. Jamison submitted her resignation from the Christian education board. Two weeks later, James Hawthorne said he was really too busy with his plumbing business to serve on the board any longer. Then someone mentioned that Dr. Thompson had not attended the last several Christian education meetings. What was going on? Were these people really overworked? Why weren't they enjoying this ministry? The pastor thought the chairman, Roy Blaylock, was doing a fine job. Pastor and Roy always met before each C.E. board meeting to review the agenda. Roy asked the pastor what he wanted in terms of solutions to problems and appointments of teachers. The pastor usually had some good ideas, since he spent more time around the church than anyone else. The pastor, therefore, did not attend the C.E. meetings. But when Roy presented the matters for consideration he always presented them in a way that let all of the members know that the pastor had already made the decisions.

Really, that was not the case. The pastor recognized the need for others to exercise their gifts and abilities. He did not intend to railroad the meeting in absentia. His discussion with Roy prior to each meeting was only to supply input and information from his perspective. He never intended to be a dictator over the board. Yet Roy perceived that whatever the pastor suggested must be accepted and approved. Naturally the other members of the committee resented spending their time in a meeting where decisions had already been made prior to that gathering. Soon these qualified people felt as though they were unnecessary because they were serving only as rubber stamps. Frustrated, they began bailing out.

The pastor could have complained that the committee members were unfaithful, that they lacked commitment to the church, to Christian education, or to the Lord. But he wisely started digging into the circumstances to find the underlying problem. When he discovered what was really happening, he was able to restructure his meetings with Roy. He explained the true perspective of his input into the committee. That solved the problem.

A pastor friend of mine told me that his church had seemed to be operating in love and unity when he was a candidate to be the pastor, but soon after he arrived he realized that one certain woman was the cause of much dissension. Her sins were gossiping, bickering, and backbiting. As the new pastor talked with several church leaders about the matter, he discovered that this woman had been disrupting the work of God in that small church for many years. The pastor then brought the matter before the official church board and asked that they take some action to correct the situation. The men sat in silence. When the pastor gently pushed to discover the reason for their apathy, one man spoke for the group. "Pastor, you will one day leave this community and go to another church. But we have to live here with that woman." How sad that the entire church had to endure a two-edged tongue in order to keep a semblance of peace. The underlying problem in that situation was not just the woman, but the irresponsible behavior of the church leaders.

Sometimes the underlying problem is with relationships. Some people do not work well together. That was the problem in the primary department. Jane Moorhead was a fine and gracious Christian lady. She seemed to be spiritually motivated, and she loved the primary children. Yet it was difficult to find people who would stay long in her department. She was an excellent teacher, and she was faithful to the work of the Lord. For these reasons, she had been promoted from primary teacher to primary department superintendent a year previously. But a close look at the situation revealed that Jane was not a good supervisor. Her lack of organization disqualified her to lead the teachers in the department. The "Peter Principle" had been put into operation in the church. That principle (see the book *The Peter Principle*, by Laurence J. Peter and Raymond Hull, William Morrow & Co., New York, 1969) declares that when a person does well in one capacity, organizations tend to continue promoting him until he reaches his level of incompetency, and there he stays. Good teachers do not always make good superintendents. A good usher does not always make a good head usher. Choir members may not be qualified or gifted to be choir directors.

At one time we could not get people to stay in our church nursery and care for the babies. We tried to motivate people in a positive way by telling them that the nursery is a ministry. Then we tried begging people. We even thought about threatening people. Nothing seemed to work. After a while we started paying people to stay in the nursery. Even then, problems continued. After some frustration, the official board researched the problem. It did not take the researchers long to realize that the major difficulty was the facilities of the nursery. The room lacked ventilation. The supplies were insufficient. The place needed more shelves and drawers. The children needed a carpet on which to play. The area was so crowded that the workers were constantly frustrated trying to care for the children. The point is that sometimes the underlying problem is simply mechanical and may be solved by moving, equipping, remodeling or rearranging.

"I'm sorry," apologized the chairman of the Rocky Mountain Security Fund to Pastor Harper, "but we cannot approve your request for a loan." I was part of that committee which voted not to lend money to the applying church for a new building. We had established the security fund a few years before in order to help small churches like Pastor Harper's, that could not get loans elsewhere. So far, we had been quite successful in selling bonds and supplying low-interest loans to smaller churches. Pastor Harper was leading his church into a building program in a new section of town. The church had big plans. They believed that when they had a new building in a new residential area, there would be immediate growth. But the truth was, the church had not grown much at all in the past. There was no guarantee that a new building was going to help the situation in any appreciable manner.

In checking the reasons for that church's lack of growth, it became evident that Pastor Harper believed he was the only one doing the ministry. He was indeed a kind and gracious man. He was an acceptable preacher, according to most people, and he was an extremely hard worker. He was even willing to drive a schoolbus to supplement his income. He was always on call for any of his flock. He loved his people and served them faithfully. But he did not know how to delegate responsibilities. He was unsuccessful at training others. He saw himself as doing the ministry and serving the people while others simply sat and watched. In this situation, the underlying problem was not relational or mechanical, it was theological.

The church growth movement centering at Fuller Seminary constantly exhorts church leaders to discover whether the underlying reason for a church's not growing is that it doesn't want to grow. Perhaps the people are comfortable with the size church they currently have. Maybe they don't see a need to grow. The truth is that these kinds of underlying problems must be identified before a church can plan its procedures and institute change.

Discover the Power Structure.
"Nothing happens in this church unless John Powers gives his approval," the new pastor was told. It is rare that a new pastor gets such good data. Usually he must discover the power structure on his own. It really isn't too difficult, though. The power in the church may be held by one who doesn't even have an official position. Usually power is best recognized by its ability to veto. Those with power usually exercise the power of veto more frequently than the power to pull together coalitions and actually get things done.

The church leader who wants to create change in an orderly fashion from within the church must discover who has that kind of power in the local church. You may discover that power rests in the hands of a few people. Perhaps power is concentrated in one or two families or groups, or perhaps in a certain committee.

Unfortunately power often is related to money, even in the church. Frequently people believe that those who control the checkbook control the ministry. But a close look at the practice of Jesus Christ shows what he thought about that kind of power structure. Do you remember who the treasurer of the twelve was? That's right, it was Judas Iscariot. Judas, the betrayer, was the one who held the power over the money. Jesus, of course, knew that Judas would betray him. Yet he allowed him to have that particular power. Evidently Jesus did not relate ministry and money in the power structure.

Some people may object to talking about a power structure at all in the church. But it is naive to suggest that a power structure does not exist in every church. Where you have people, you have a power structure. Even in the most spiritual church, where Jesus Christ is considered to be the head of the church, a power structure still exists among the people. I know one fine church where the pastor maintains that he is not the senior minister. He simply considers himself one of the elders. He tells others that he is not *the* leader of the church, but *a* leader of the church. Yet, anyone who really understands the in-working of that church will tell you that, when the elders sit around the table in a meeting, this man in effect has at least two votes while everyone else has only one.

It may not seem spiritual to talk about the power structure, but it is necessary for anyone who wants to create change. As you look closely at the relationship of Jesus' twelve disciples, you will see a power structure there. There also was a very evident power structure in the beginning church as it is recorded in Acts. Even in the pastoral epistles, Paul makes it very clear that some wield authority over others in the church.

Power is granted by the people. That is true in any situation in life. Not only within our form of government but even in a dictatorship, the ruler governs ultimately by the will of the people. Temporarily he may govern only because he has the guns and tanks, but if the people become dissatisfied enough with his rule, they will rebel and he will rule no more.

The same is true in the church. Usually the power people within a church are those who have been hard workers with long tenure. It may be that their money has been an influence also. But mostly those with power have gained it through the honorable means of being willing to serve and being faithful in their responsibilities. Most often those with power in the local assembly have earned their way to that position.

One problem which must be recognized is that some people have power by reason of their relationship. Spouses especially must be cautious not to exercise undue power over their mates who hold positions in the church. And office holders must be cautious not to reveal confidences to their spouses. For example, a wife probably wields more influence over her husband than any other person on earth. It is only natural that, as he talks about certain circumstances and she makes suggestions, he will respect her words and perhaps try to institute those suggestions. Of course, the suggestions may be right and proper, but the couple must realize that the wife is still only one person in the congregation. And she, too, works from a bagful of pressures and prejudices just like everyone else.

Often leaders realize that it is desirable in a church that the power be spread among many people. But wait a minute! Think that one through carefully. Remember that the power to make decisions also carries the power to veto. Until the leader wanting to create orderly change can build relationships and develop mature leaders, he may do better in not having so many people share the power. Certainly the best approach is for the church to operate with many people each taking a chunk of the power pie. But until that can be done properly, it may be a mistake to do it at all. The leader may simply create more headaches and time traps for himself if he must go to ten people or ten committees instead of simply working with the current one committee and two people who hold power in the church.

Says Alec MacKenzie in *The Time Trap*:

Management teaches us about the power pie. How much power does my department have in the company? How much power do I have in my own department? Imagine for a moment that I am your boss; you are a member of my team. If I keep control of every decision, the power pie is all mine. If I decentralize our decision-making, then I share the power pie with you. When the power pie is cut more ways, the boss' share does not get smaller; it gets larger. The whole pie grows. If a manager permits his subordinates to exercise influence on what goes on in his department, does he have correspondingly less influence? The research of management sociologist, Rensis Likert, says, "No."[17]

When a major purchase was being considered by a church, a godly leader of that church was opposed. He had always held veto power in that church. He was a faithful, hardworking Christian who had seen the church through some dark days. He wasn't usually pushy, but this time he felt strongly that the church should not make the purchase it was considering. The cost of the purchase was not the problem. The money was available. He just felt that the church was spending too freely and a line had to be drawn somewhere. This is where he decided to make his stand. He frankly talked with the pastor and others who were in favor of the purchase. This man and the pastor agreed to disagree agreeably. The consideration went through the proper channels and was approved over the negative vote of this opposer. That was a hard blow to him. Never before had the church voted against this church leader on a major issue.

As a church grows, those who formerly held power may tend to lose their influence. One person can greatly influence the votes of a congregation of fifty but he has less influence over a congregation of five hundred. And as a church grows, people do not know all of the power people. When a church was small, the power people were highly visible, but as it grew and undertook multiple Sunday morning services, the "up front" leaders gained a disproportionate amount of power.

"Susan doesn't really have the quality of voice that we want for Sunday morning solos. Maybe we should not put her on the new schedule for special music anymore." Thus a power person quietly used his influence to move someone out of a position of ministry. The real reason Hank opposed Susan was that she had rebuffed his romantic advances. Susan is a widow and Hank's wife died several years ago. Hank was interested but Susan wasn't. And now Hank has (perhaps even unconsciously) evened the score. The point is that leaders must be cautious not to use their power in the wrong way. Leaders have a great responsibility to help others find places of ministry in the body. This responsibility applies even toward those who have opposed them and to those they do not particularly appreciate. It is also possible that those who constitute the "inner circle" get the contracts for the painting, plumbing, and fencing when the new building comes along. That too can be a misuse of power.

It may take a little effort to discover who holds power. It is surprising to learn that those with great power often do not tip their hand with outward behavior. Frequently the power people in the church are not the talkative, boisterous ones. Many times the one with power walks softly but carries a big stick. He has learned that he can direct affairs by simply raising an eyebrow or placing a question. People know how to act and how to vote when the power person lets his opinion be made known. Please do not misunderstand and get the impression that power people are all devious, dangerous, greedy people. It is not wrong for people to have power. The truth is that power must rest in someone wherever a group of people relate to one another. Some member of each committee must help the committee with its project and purpose. Frequently the elected chairman is not the one with the real power. The power person often sits quietly and directs the committee from the middle of the table rather than from the head of it. Remember that there is nothing wrong in such an approach. The problem is not that individuals have power; the problem exists only when individuals misuse power.

Since power people often do not have a high visibility, the one trying to lead the church into creative change will have to look carefully to determine where the real power is. Sometimes the power is in the barely visible wife of an office holder. Sometimes the power abides in an elderly person who does not always attend the church services. And in some cases the power of a church is in a denominational leader who rarely is visible on Sunday. Even denominations whose churches boast of being independent may in reality have a denominational leader who is only a state director or coordinator, but who really wields a great amount of power in several churches under his influence.

"Mike Tucker ... umm, haven't you applied and been accepted to our seminary for next fall? We will be looking forward to having you as a student. What?! You are going to that other seminary which is nondenominational? Well, Mike, you must realize that, when it comes time for ordination, all of those kinds of matters will be carefully considered."

With these solemn words, a seminary president tried to coerce me, when I was a college senior, into attending his school. It is interesting to note that those who have power in certain contexts of life often try to misuse that power and abuse people in other spheres of life. This denominational school president had absolutely no right of authority over me. Yet he threatened to put my future ordination in jeopardy. Little did he know that some of us are absolutely revolted by such denominational politics and that, after his remarks, wild horses could not have dragged me to his school.

More recently a former college professor was in town and gave me a call. We had an amiable conversation. He invited me to attend the meetings he was holding in our city. I thanked him politely. As we neared the end of our conversation, he again reminded me of the meetings and concluded his remarks with, "We will see you one night this week." Well, he did not see me any night that week, or since then. I considered his subtlety a misuse of power. Such situations occur among God's people. Sometimes an older Christian will try to use his power against a younger Christian. One of the great experiences of my life was growing up in a church and later joining that church staff. I was in charge of the ministry of young people. The couple assisting in this area was the same couple who had ministered to young people when I was in high school. They graciously accepted my authority over them. Not once did they use their power of years and former authority to try to sway that ministry. Frankly, had they come on very strong, I would have accepted whatever they suggested because of my love and respect for them. But they never did that.

A church which has a number of relatives in the places of authority may encounter trouble. The one with the power in the family will be tempted to use that same power to influence his relatives in the church. A similar problem may occur when the church membership consists largely of those who work in the same office or plant. The one who is the boss at work may also be seen as the one with the most power at the church. And he may not be the most qualified in spiritual matters.

One of my first impressions of the church where I now minister came when I was a candidate for the pastorate. We were eating a meal together at the church on that Sunday afternoon. I remember Bob's displaying obvious power over Ralph, another of the church leaders. Both seemed content with the situation. Neither expressed any unkindness or jealousy to the other. Yet I learned at the end of the afternoon that Ralph was a full colonel in the Air Force and Bob was a sergeant. In a military community such as ours, we must constantly be careful that military rank is not an acceptable way to divide the power in the church. Neither is it acceptable to distribute power according to a person's educational degrees or status in the community. The mayor of the city, by virtue of his office in the community, has no more inherent power in the house of God than anyone else.

Educate/Propagate/Diffuse Information.

What is the church supposed to be doing? That is a big question indeed. Already we have mentioned that when God's people was Israel, they were also a political entity who knew what they should be doing. But frankly, most Christians don't understand the nature and function of the church. When asked or observed, most people demonstrate that they believe the church is the place to attend meetings and hear preaching. Most Christians have the idea that someone is supposed to be helping other people become Christians. And probably the majority of Christians agree that somewhere, somehow, we are to love one another and send missionaries to fields abroad.

One of the first tasks of the Christian who wants to create orderly change within the church is to educate people about the church. However, several young ministers I know have made the mistake of leaving seminary and preaching their first series of sermons on the nature of the church. Usually churches are not ready to hear those truths from their new minister. The wise pastor will spend his first months in a new pastorate building the saints and establishing rapport with those in power. After he is known and appreciated as one who ministers to the flock, then he can move on to the important task of educating about the church.

Yesterday Jon dropped a sheaf of papers on my desk. The stack represented a proposal that we hire a building inspector/coordinator. The proposal was in rough draft before it went to the secretary to be typed and duplicated for distribution at our board meeting later that evening. The proposal was well done and thorough. It explained whom Jon was suggesting be hired for this position. It included an adequate review of the man's qualifications, experience, and education. It also included a job description. The cost of the new position was indicated adequately for where we were with the proposal. But there was a glaring error in the arrangement of the material. The reason that we needed such a person was buried in the middle of the proposal. "Before that goes to the board," I suggested, "why don't you put the reasons for this position as the first paragraph?" Jon followed my suggestion, and the board accepted the proposal with little discussion.

It never ceases to amaze me when I realize that a church board will spend $10,000 with five minutes' discussion and, on another occasion, will hassle for an hour over a $9.95 item. The difference usually is in the preparation and education that have taken place with the presentation of the need. Any change you think ought to take place in your church must begin with education. Tell why the change is needed, why the purchase is necessary, why the personnel are required. Show cause first.

It is not enough to state as a reason for home Bible studies that others are doing it. Demonstrate to the power people that the approach is biblical and that it gets results. Deliver the facts. Talk with those who have enjoyed such studies. Invite some of the power people to attend such a study. Educate the leadership.

One principle of educating leaders in order to create change is to take matters slowly. Several weeks after I spoke at a pastors' retreat, I saw a young minister who had attended the retreat. He greeted me with the news that he had taken most of our church's innovations and dumped them on his board—all at once. "Mike," he told me, "they just looked at me and shook their heads as if to say, 'Don't ever try any of that foolishness around here.'" His church is trying to change. But his problem was "too much too soon," and his leaders choked.

Another principle which seems to contradict the first is to keep the challenge constantly before the people you wish to educate and change. Create change slowly, but keep at it. Many church leaders are bored with the simplistic way the church operates. In our advanced space age, too many churches still operate the way they did years ago in rural America. They lack basic business-management skills that would improve efficiency. They fail to keep people awake because they lack vision to challenge them.

For some time I have been working on changing the entire structure of our church. The new proposal, I believe, is more in line with New Testament principles. This is probably the most thoroughgoing change a church could ever anticipate. Because of the magnitude of the change, I have been going very slowly. I have talked with most of the leaders of the church about the change. I have been in Bible studies and conversations for over a year to get the feedback that is necessary. Finally, it was time to make a presentation of the matter. So I wrote a paper and distributed it to our official board. Since we meet every week, not much time elapsed between the distribution and the presentation. The paper was distributed one week with the request to read it so that we could discuss it the following week. The following week there was almost no discussion. The changes I proposed were so major that the entire constitution would have to be discarded and a new one written in its place. Yet there I sat surrounded in silence. The changes were already accepted by our board. After a few moments of that enjoyable silence, I moved to some new areas of challenge. These were challenges I had been thinking about but had not dared to explore quite yet. At that meeting, I was even able to move into the area of challenging the necessity for such a lengthy doctrinal statement in our constitution. I was not challenging the doctrine, only the need to have it written in our constitution the way it presently appeared. That gave the board something else to think about.

Another principle is: be honest. Educate without manipulating people to your point of view. Be willing to be shot out of the saddle. Whenever I have a red-hot idea that needs attention, I begin to bounce it off different people of the church. I unload the idea and ask for honest evaluation. The people I communicate with in this manner know they have the freedom to be critical, brutally critical if necessary. I appreciate that. I'm not trying to win them over to my way of thinking. I'm not trying to persuade them at this point. I'm asking for evaluation.

By the time I bring my "world-changing plan" to the board or committee involved, I have probably seen at least half of the people individually. I do not see them individually in order to "stack the committee" with my idea or manipulate people to vote for the new approach. But by the time I meet with the whole group, I know most of their feelings and thoughts about the idea. I know their criticisms, and I have been able to work on solutions. My idea has been burned and beaten and reformed. If I still think it is valid, it is by that time refined enough to stand the further evaluation of the whole committee. Usually the original idea has been enhanced by suggestions and deletions of the individuals I tried it out on prior to the committee meeting. However, I must realize that the idea may still be wrong at this time, for this situation, for this place. I can't go to the committee with the thought of winning them over to my side. God leads through people on committees and boards too, not just through a few leaders.

Many times I've been glad that I didn't bully a group to follow my suggestions. In our educational building there stands a wall that I opposed. I thought building that wall was unnecessary and too expensive. But the building committee disagreed and built it anyway. I can see now that they were right; I was wrong. Without the wall, we would lose the efficiency of three classrooms.

Evaluate Feedback.

"Everyone is unhappy with the new youth minister." "Our kids love the new youth minister. He is an answer to prayer." "No one likes the new primary curriculum." "The organ playing while the pastor prays is disturbing." "She shouldn't be allowed to solo in our church again. Her style just doesn't fit here." "We love that soloist. She really ministers to our whole family." An active group will give plenty of feedback. The problem is how to evaluate it.

First, be cautious not to accept too small a portion. Even feedback from important power people may not give you a true reading on what is happening in the church. Remember, too, not to place too much emphasis on the evaluation of even your own husband or wife. Always try to find out the source of your informer's information. If he comes and says that people are unhappy with the couple who are working with the junior high, then ask with whom he talked. Ask how many people he talked with. Try to get as many facts as you can. Return and interview original sources.

One church always set an attendance goal for its Easter services. That church was not an attendance-oriented church. The only time they ever set a goal was for Easter. They never had contests or tried to hustle people to meetings. But somehow the tradition had gotten started of having a large Easter service and setting an attendance goal for that service. On one occasion, the pastor asked the congregation on a Sunday morning prior to Easter what they thought this year's goal should be. He enthusiastically reported the goals which had been broken for the past several Easters. Yet, when he asked the congregation for feedback, there was deafening silence. He was embarrassed, and so was the congregation. The fact was that no one was really interested in attendance goals after all. Finally, someone asked as kindly as possible, "Why should we have an attendance goal this year?" The pastor did not have an adequate answer. In some instances individual feedback before public presentation would greatly enhance a presentation or spare the leader from embarrassment.

Always obtain your feedback from a cross section of the congregation. When you evaluate the new pianist, ask nonmusicians as well as musicians and song leaders. When evaluating the new format used on Sunday evening, ask the teen-agers as well as the power people. When you evaluate a teacher, ask his students as well as his colleagues. Attendance alone may not give adequate feedback on a teacher.

The senior pastor was visibly upset. Three elders had reported that the assistant pastor was so badly mishandling his responsibilities of visitation and counseling that he must be dismissed from the church staff. All three elders cited examples of visitors who had attended the church and had never been contacted. Two of the elders believed the assistant pastor had given bad advice to women in the church whose husbands were not Christians. These three power people stated that many others in the congregation were upset also. The wise senior minister listened carefully and asked penetrating questions. He tried to discover the sources of information. He sought out how many people were actually involved in the unhappiness. Finally he suggested that all four of them confront the young assistant. The confrontation was not to be an accusation, but simply a report of what they had heard. The young minister was shaking by the time the elders finished giving him their list, but he acted in a mature manner by answering each objection. The result was a mutual realization that the assistant was not handling some areas and some people in the proper way. When the elders pointed that out to him, he agreed to change. Much of the information was misinformation. When the elders saw that, they discounted it. Their first impulse was to fire him, but wisdom and patience led to reconciliation. Don't make an evaluation until you have adequate feedback.

Set Goals.

In your church you want to create orderly change from within. Let's suppose that the current situation is that you are a member in good standing of a typical evangelical church. The problem is that you do not sense that there is sufficient life and purposeful activity in the church. You have few young people; most of the members are elderly. You find little excitement about what is going on. Members demonstrate a decent amount of faithfulness to the church and its service, but few visitors are attracted to the meetings. Your church buildings are adequate, but in poor repair. Most of the members do not even notice that several walls need painting and several pew cushions are coming apart. Floor tiles are missing in some classrooms. The present pastor has been in the church for two years. He is a middle-aged man who had had three or four pastorates before this one. His speaking ability is not superb, but he isn't too terribly boring. He is a kind man who seems to love the people and is available when he is needed. All in all, he is judged a fairly competent minister.

The attendance at your church leveled off at 125 in the morning services about five years ago. A few people have joined since then, but several families have moved away, so the average stays about the same. A year ago you tried a visitation program that had been widely acclaimed as the answer to the need to reach more people, but the few who were involved in the training lost interest and the program faltered. Besides, the program was built upon the basis of visiting non-Christians who had been in your church the previous Sunday — and frankly, few non-Christians ever attend your church at all.

Just a few months ago, your church cooperated with a city-wide evangelistic campaign. Many churches worked together to try an entirely new approach based upon mass-media saturation and telephone surveys. During the course of that campaign, several people received Christ as Savior as the result of some of your church members' talking with them. But these telephone conversations never materialized further and none of the new converts ever attended your church. The week after the campaign was finished, the church was in the same old rut.

The underlying problem, as you see it, is a need for new people in the church. You see a need for an excitement about the Christian life and the work of God through his church. You see a need to stimulate Christians to reach others for Christ.

Two of the elders in the church seem to be the power people. Both are good men who have been in the church for many years. Both now say that they are tired of the burden of responsibility that has been theirs, though they were especially helpful the last two times the church was without a pastor. It seemed then that they rose to the occasion and took responsibility in a new and dynamic way.

Certainly the present pastor is an individual with influence in the church. He is well liked and could certainly be considered as one of those with power. But some have suspected that he is looking around and that he may leave the church soon for another ministry.

Another person with some power is a young man who has just started teaching an adult class. This class, which reaches twenty- to forty-year-olds, is not very large, but the people seem to like Sam Bradley very much. Sam is in a middle-management position with his company. He moved to your city six months ago. When he bought a home near the church, he and his family got involved in the church almost immediately.

Perhaps you also see yourself as an individual with some power in the church. Your idea is that, to help solve the underlying problems, the church could rent and show Christian films in the homes of members. You want to suggest that the church projector be loaned to various families who would invite their neighbors in to see a good film which will lead to a natural presentation of the gospel. Your idea is that the church would finance the whole project. Members would be taught how to operate the projector and how to lead a discussion after the film. Each family or individual would be encouraged to serve refreshments after the film and attempt to present the gospel to the guests. In cooperation with the whole project, some would be on a prayer team. Perhaps some would not want to show the film, but would be willing to pray for those who do.

Your first step was to talk with the pastor and the two elders who seem to be leaders in the church. As you talked with them, you listened to their ideas too, and obtained ideas from them. They made several good suggestions, but they were not overly enthusiastic about the project. After all, nothing else had worked very well, so why should this approach? Doggedly you talked with Sam Bradley about the idea. Sam was more receptive. In fact he seemed enthusiastic. As you talked with others, you got mixed responses. No one seemed to think the project was absolutely without any merit, so you presented the whole matter to the board of elders, who invited you to visit the board meeting and to make your pitch. By the day of the presentation, all of the elders had heard about the project and you had talked personally with most of them. You approached some women of the church and asked for their comments and suggestions. You carefully considered older members in the discussions also. In the board meeting, as you continued to talk about the project, enthusiasm seemed to increase. Already you had checked to make sure the church's projector was in good repair. It needed an extra projection lamp and you were willing to buy that yourself. The local Christian film distributor suggested several excellent films for such use. Now people were beginning to make commitments to show the films in their homes and invite their neighbors.

Now you are ready to set your goal. What do you expect to accomplish with this approach? Certainly one goal is to guide people to receive Christ as Savior. Another goal is to encourage people to be active in evangelism. A further goal is to get the new converts incorporated into the body of Christ. You may even see that one of your goals is to contact Christians who are not involved in any other church. The approach may help them get their lives in line with the will of God. Another goal is that this experiment will lead to other creative ways to reach people for Christ and cause your entire church to grow.

Chapter six deals with the matter of promoting big goals. The point here is that setting goals helps us keep going and reaching for new goals. Goals stimulate, activate, and keep us growing as individuals and as Christians.

When I reached my five-hundredth mile on the jogging track at the local YMCA, I told my friends I was going to retire. But the next day I was back on the track reaching for 1,000 miles. Reaching one goal encouraged me to reach for another. When I reached the 1,000-mile goal on the chart, I again quipped that I'd endured enough suffering for any man. But the next day, once more, I hit the track and I've been running ever since.

Vonda Kay VanDyke, a former Miss America, says, "When I was in college, one of my favorite quotes was, 'A low man sees a little thing and does it, but a high man with a great thing to pursue dies ere he knows it.' " In other words, you can set all sorts of little goals for yourself, little accomplishments, and you can make them. But they really don't matter that much. It is different when you set a goal so high that you don't think you can reach it. Maybe you can never reach it in your lifetime, but that's what makes life exciting. Whether you make your goal or not, it's the reaching out for something that's important.

Establish Methods.

Effective leadership is an art and a science. It is an art because it involves some God-given, innate abilities. It is a science because it involves learned skills. The art of leadership deals with what you are. In Numbers 16, Moses shows us part of what a leader is. In that chapter Moses is having a confrontation with Korah. God warned Korah, through Moses, that he should not oppose his chosen leader. Korah continued to oppose Moses, however, so God opened up the earth and swallowed up the complainer. Then God sent fire from heaven and more were killed. The next day, according to verse 41, the people came and complained against Moses, saying he had killed the people. God said to Moses, "Move over. I'll finish the job." But Moses fell on his face and asked God not to kill the people. Moses was a man of compassion.

That's part of what a leader must be. In his book, *The Velvet Covered Brick*, the author says, "Leadership is not something you do, it is something you are."[18] True. But the science of leadership deals with what you do.

Of course, some people misunderstand what leadership is supposed to do. In *Charismatic Political Leadership*, author Willner lists eight characteristics that are common to effective leaders:

1. Exposure to varied environments and norms.
2. The ability to identify with the group they serve.
3. A high energy level.
4. Presence of mind or composure under conditions of stress or challenge.
5. Unswerving dedication to their goals.
6. The ability to project the impression of powerful mind and range of knowledge.
7. A capacity for innovation and originality.
8. Identification with the continuity of tradition and the proclamation of a new and different order to come.[19]

President Eisenhower was known to define leadership as getting things done through people. But how do you establish your message for such a goal? In his book, *Up the Organization*, Robert Townsend says:

Leaders come in all ages, shapes, sizes, and conditions. Some are poor administrators; some are not overly bright. One clue: since most people *per se* are mediocre, the true leader can be recognized because somehow or other his people consistently turn in superior performances.[20]

The closest we seem to be able to come to a broadly acceptable definition of leadership is: it is that which leaders do. Then, when we try to define a leader, about all the agreement is that leaders lead. Perhaps in despair over defining, we try to picture it in terms of style. In using such a broad term, we are attempting to describe how the person operates rather than what he is. If you think about a number of leaders you know personally, you can probably come up with your own summation of their style or methods. "He's a player-coach kind of guy." Or, "She's a prima donna." Or, "He's a one-man show." In other words, we tend to characterize a leader by the way he leads and the methods he uses, or by personal perception of him or her. It follows that one person may feel differently from another about a leader's style. Style turns out to be the summation of how the leader goes about carrying out his leadership functions and leading the group toward change.

You can identify several styles of leadership. One is *bureaucratic*. This is a style marked by a continual reference to organization, rules, and regulations. Bureaucratic leaders assume that somehow difficulties can be ironed out if everyone will abide by the rules. Under this style of leadership, decisions come about through parliamentary procedure. The bureaucratic leader is a diplomat who learns how to use the majority as a way to get people to perform. Here is the pastor who hides behind the committee. Decision making is always passed to another board. Here is the leader who has memorized the constitution, and clubs everyone with it. Here is the leader who knows that the finance committee and the nominating committee are the two most important places to put his "own people." The leader who uses the bureaucratic style of leadership slips people in and out of positions in the church through committee action. He doesn't confront or rebuke or affirm others. He uses the system to his advantage.

The book *New Ways of Managing Conflict* says:

Since the parliamentary procedure and *Roberts Rules of Order* are widely used today in dealing with conflict, their capacity to achieve consensus and win—win solutions—deserves to be examined. As a rule, parliamentary procedures structure an interaction into a win-lose relationship. The rigidity of a formal motion with changes possible only by an amendment makes the orderly problem-solving steps required for the search and discovery of a mutually acceptable solution difficult, if not impossible. The parliamentary struggle is a confrontation between alternative solutions already formulated. Arguing from a fixed position rules out the possibility of innovative ideas generated by the systematic search for them in a free and open manner. In the heat of argument, bruising statements may be made which never are entirely forgotten or forgiven.[21]

Another leadership style may be termed the *permissive* approach. Keeping people happy is the name of the game. It is assumed that if people feel good about themselves and others, the organization will function and the job will get done. Coordination often suffers under this style. Furthermore, the passive leader often contradicts himself. He is so intent on pleasing others that he says what each person wants to hear. That eventually means that he tells one person one thing and another person gets a contradictory statement.

Another style—the *participative* style—is popular today. This is used by those who believe the way to motivate others is to involve them in the decision-making process. This hopefully creates mutual goal ownership and a feeling of shared purpose. Here the problem is inaction or delay in times of crisis. Also, the power-hungry individual will attempt to take over from the one who uses a participative style of leadership. Have you ever tried to teach by using the discussion method and then been frustrated when one person attempts to grab the reins from you and teach the class?

The *autocratic* leadership style is frequently used in evangelical churches. This is marked by reliance upon authority, usually assuming that people will not do anything unless they are told. It discourages innovation. The leader sees himself as indispensable. He believes he is God's man in God's place, and everyone else should recognize that and do what he says. The advantage is, of course, that decisions can be made quickly with this style. As a *World Vision* article says:

It is important to realize that leaders will need different styles at different times. The appropriate style depends a great deal upon the task of the organization, the phase of life of the organization, and the needs of the moment.[22]

The very task that a youth leader or a choir director must perform demands that sometimes he take an autocratic approach to leadership. Sometimes the choir director must simply say in practice, "Here is the note to be hit. Here is the way we will sing this arrangement." That may not be the time for a participative committee to meet and decide. A church leader must sometimes direct ushers in carrying out their task. At five minutes until eleven o'clock, as people pour into the auditorium, it is not the time to use the bureaucratic or permissive approach of telling ushers that they must set chairs in the aisle.

Churches also go through different phases. During periods of rapid growth and expansion, autocratic leadership may work very well. For example, the founding pastor of a church is often a good leader who knows intuitively what needs to be done and how to do it. Since the vision is his, he is best able to impart it to others without a discussion. But during periods of slow growth or of consolidation, the organization needs to be much more reflective to attempt to be more efficient. Participative leadership may then be the order of the day.

Both of these considerations need to be tempered by the need of the moment. Using autocratic leadership may work well for fighting fires (either real or figurative ones), but it will be less successful in dealing with a personal problem.

It follows that, ideally, a leader should have many different styles. He should be a man for all seasons, shifting from the permissive mood of summer to the demands of winter. What kind of leadership does your church need at *this* time? What is its task? What phase of organizational growth are you in? What is the specific situation? Analyze this with help from your board, your leadership team, your power people, your church members.

What kind of leader are you? What styles do you use? Review your calendar of meetings for the last few weeks. What happened in those meetings? Did you go to those meetings just to announce your decision, autocratic-style? Did you go with a hidden agenda, expecting only to get the concurrence of the group? Did you go expecting to work with the group to arrive at a decision, participative style? Did you go expecting to sit back and let others worry about the problem, permissive-style? Or did you go intending to use the parliamentary procedure to make sure that the ship stayed on an even keel, bureaucratic-style? If you discover that you handled each meeting in the same way, you are probably too locked into one style; you should consider modifying your style according to the current situation. By deciding before the meeting which style you will adopt, you will give yourself the advantage of being able to observe the response of the other members of the meeting, and you will be a better leader who helps to create orderly change in the church.

Talk About Change.

The Church That Dared to Change placed us on the evangelical circuit of those doing research into the matter of renewal and church growth. Frequently people come to Colorado Springs to interview us and discover our "secret." But after people finish their tour, which usually includes Circle Church in Chicago, Our Heritage Wesleyan in Scottsdale, and Peninsula Bible Church in Palo Alto, they may be more confused than ever. The fact is that each church that is growing has learned to minister to its own locale in its own way.

A frustration I have endured since this interviewing began is the question people always ask about our goals. "What are your measurable goals?" The emphasis is always on *measurable*. That is a tough question. One can measure attendance and finances, but how do you measure spiritual growth in an individual or church? And surely spiritual growth is our primary goal. We believe and preach that our primary goal is to help people toward maturity in Christ.

We use three methods to accomplish that goal: evangelism (helping people receive Christ as Savior), discipleship (helping people have a personal, daily walk with Christ), and training (helping people serve the Lord). One can measure the success of such a goal by watching and observing how many people receive Christ, how many say that they have a personal walk with God, and how many get involved in ministries. But the problem is, people can fake it! I don't really know if anyone else in the world is actually walking with the Lord or not. Participation in Bible studies, prayer and other behavior can give me a hint; the absence of those activities may tell me that an individual is *not* walking with

God. But he can do all those things, and still be far from the Lord in attitude, spirit, and heart. The same is true with ministry. How many Sunday school teachers take their teaching assignment merely so they won't feel guilty? How many sing in the choir because they like to sing anywhere, not really realizing that singing in the choir is a spiritual ministry? No one can answer those questions.

So, how does one measure spiritual growth? How can we really know if we are meeting our goals? That was an annoying question. But not any more. It finally occurred to us that *our goal is really the process*. Since we realized that no one ever reaches ultimate maturity in Christ this side of heaven, we must all be going through the process of maturity now. So our goal is not an ultimate standard of behavior, but the process of moving toward it. In other words, we no longer measure our success by looking for a product. If suddenly George Platte stops beating his wife, we are happy, of course, but that isn't our success. Our success is that we helped institute a process that God used to work on George's life so that his behavior changed. Are we putting the process into action and making it available? Or are we not? If we are, then we are meeting our goal. What God does with the process is entirely his business. When we formally launch a program we need to remember that the goal is for this new program (or adaptation of an old program) to become a process whereby people will be helped toward maturity in Christ.

Keeping the idea of change before the congregation is valuable. People like to see movement and progress. If changes just slip by quietly, some people will not notice. Those heavily involved in the life of the church are often startled to discover that when rather significant changes occurred, many other people did not observe the changes. One easy way to illustrate that the church is interested in innovation and change is to lead the way with a central meeting of the church. Regardless of how much a church tries to emphasize fellowship, singing, evangelism, Sunday school, or any other good ingredient of church life, the central focus for most people is still the Sunday morning service.

And certain simple changes that take place during that hour can set the tone and raise the standard for change throughout the entire church.

How about just changing the order of the service? Delete or include a few hymns. Try an overhead projector in preaching, in giving announcements, or in teaching a new hymn. Have the soloist sing *after* the message. Put the special music at the very beginning. Kneel for prayer (don't kneel if that is your custom). Have the choir stand in a different place. Rearrange the pulpit furniture. Remove the pulpit. Move the organ. Give announcements from a different place. Start the offering plates from the back of the auditorium. Use a different type of offertory. Drop the offertory and encourage people to talk to one another. Omit or insert a formal prayer, or have a time of quiet meditation. Omit or insert the reading of Scripture. Give announcements from offstage so people hear as the speaker talks into a microphone, but they do not see. The same can be done with a soloist. People will listen better, at least for a while. But when that device is overused, the congregation will listen no better to announcements than they do now. Maybe none of these suggestions appeal to you. Perhaps you have tried all of these and are beyond this list. Never mind, the point is that a little creativity in that morning service will shout to the people, "We are open to change in this church."

The first Sunday of each quarter is a time of excitement and change around our church. That's the time we begin new adult electives. The concept is not really new or creative, but we build anticipation, and the change is fun. We announce the new courses three to four weeks in advance. We promote them through our church newspaper and bulletin. We print a sharp-looking brochure explaining each course and introducing the teachers. We ask people to sign up for the courses of their choice. We show the list on an overhead projector during the church service. When the first Sunday of each quarter comes, the people feel excitement about something new.

But be careful. Overkill is a real possibility. Sometimes we beat the drum so long and so often that people learn that the noise before the program is more exciting than the actual program. We must produce ministries of value, not just create a disturbance. And of course, change doesn't have to be introduced with balloons, prizes, gimmicks, and buttons. A contest usually generates more enthusiasm for itself than for what it is supposed to promote.

But you do need to talk about change and introduce change if people are going to get the message that change is acceptable and even desirable. When the junior highers go on a retreat, let the whole church know. When the choir gets new robes or quits wearing robes, or changes places when they sing, talk about it. The long-time members will notice (some of them will, at least), but newer people and visitors will think that's what they always wear and that's where they always stand. When you change the method of registering on Sunday morning, make the notice, "Today we want you to do something different when you register . . ." Don't manufacture talk about change and don't be guilty of overkill. But do talk about changes, large and small. When you do, you may be surprised to learn that your church really is changing more than you thought, and that alone will improve morale and create a climate for additional changes.

"We are already desegregated," I told the church I pastored in Birmingham, Alabama. It was the late 1960s and the church was going through the agony of deciding its stand on desegregation. But the truth was that the church had already admitted a Mexican who was a student at a nearby Bible college. The church never struggled over accepting this fine young man from Yucatan, Mexico. The desegregation question was simply not an issue. So, by my pointing out that the church was already desegregated, some of the emotion was drained from the issue of admitting blacks.

Some Christians fear change. It is an emotional issue. If you can demonstrate that your church already is involved in change (the more examples you can think of, the stronger will be your case), it may help those who fear to see that they only fear *certain* changes; just as the church in Alabama didn't really fear deseg-regation, they just feared blacks.

Summary.

One piece of dialogue between two thieves has helped me a great deal. The conversation came in a movie I was watching on television. The story was of a young pickpocket who was not very skilled in his chosen trade. Two professional pickpockets took him under their wings. The two older men were experts. Once when the group was staying in an expensive hotel (they always traveled first class), one of the professionals was training the young man in lifting wallets. "Wow!" exclaimed the student. "You really know how to do that well." The elderly man looked at his student in disgust, raised his eyebrows, lifted his nose, and haughtily exclaimed, "Boy, that's what I do. It's my job."

I believe that a part of the job God has given me to do is to create orderly change from within the church. But that change will not come unless I consider that it is *what I do*. It is my job. I am not speaking of myself as a pastor, but as an ordinary Christian in the church. Helpful change occurs only when someone has a burden to create it. It must be planned. Here is the procedure:

1. Recognize the current situation.
2. Define the underlying problems.
3. Locate the power structure.
4. Educate.
5. Evaluate feedback.
6. Set goals.
7. Establish methods.
8. Talk about change.

Three
PROPAGATE UNITY TO ENCOURAGE CHANGE

Singleness of Heart.

If you have the patience to observe silently and motionlessly, you'll behold amazing sights in the mangrove swamps of Australia. The swamps teem with life. Much of that life can be seen only in certain seasons or at certain times of the day. Some of that creation of God may be observed only at high or low tides. After the tides lower, one can watch some of the beaches and see hundreds of soldier crabs all emerge at once and scurry together in a great hurry toward the interior of the swamp. What a beautiful sight to see all those small creatures simultaneously move in unity!

We who believe are carefully joined together with Christ as parts of a beautiful, constantly growing temple for God. And you also are joined with him and with each other by the Spirit, and are part of this dwelling place of God (Ephesians 2:21-23).

A friend of mine played in a high school orchestra. The musicians always tuned their instruments to the nasal "A" of the oboe, but in this particular case the oboist was a joker. He sounded the wrong note. And the other players tuned to that note. The particular performance that night featured a well-known pianist. The first number began with the pianist playing a long introduction. After his lengthy introduction, beautifully performed, the orchestra was prepared to enter into the music. But when the conductor directed the first measure of music, it was obvious that something was wrong. What an awful sound came from those improperly tuned instruments!

It is not enough to arrange a group of outstanding musicians in an orchestra and tell them to play a certain score, even though the correct number of instruments is there. It is still not enough to distribute music which each had played individually before. What is needed is for each instrument to be properly tuned in relation to the other, and a leader who knows what total effect he wants. That leader must also be able to communicate his desires to each player. Unfortunately, churches are not always known for their unity. Often the church is the object of ridicule because Christians have not displayed the unity they have in Christ.

Remains of an ancient Christian civilization in the Nubian Region of the Nile Valley were found just prior to the completion of the Aswan Dam in Egypt. Pioneer archaeologists from the Roman Catholic Church found an entire cathedral with frescoes in excellent condition. The archaeologists confirmed that a Christian civilization flourished in the area from the fifth century. Islam and Christianity apparently lived side by side for many centuries. The experts think that Christianity disappeared from the area, not because of Moslem pressure but for internal reasons. How often have churches lost their testimony in communities because of a lack of unity among the members? Orderly change cannot take place in the church when there is a basic problem of disunity.

A man from our church flew on the first plane to Hanoi after the signing of the peace treaty and the agreement to return our prisoners of war. He has many stories to tell about men who had been kept captive under primitive conditions. On his way from Hanoi to Clark Air Force Base one of the pilots told him a particularly touching story. He said that after he was first shot down and taken captive, enemies led him through many villages with his hands tied tightly behind his back. Villagers shouted obscenities and hurled objects at him. But while he was being badly abused, he felt someone press an object into his hand behind his back. He closed his fingers over the object and waited. Hours later, when his hands were finally untied, he found a crumbled cookie in his hands. Then he recalled that the villager who had placed the morsel of food in his hand had caught his eye as she moved back into the crowd. When she saw him looking at her, she made a sign of the cross. There is unity in the body of Christ even when one Christian has dropped a bomb on the home of another Christian. Those who want to effect change must take advantage of the inherent unity that already exists in the hearts of God's people.

Helping people to know the goals of a church will help those people *come* together and *change* together in unity. When people truly understand why the church exists and what they should be doing as part of the church, they will be more likely to be unified in changes the leaders wish to institute. Furthermore, people must have a desire to be an integral part of the group before they will experience unity in a desire to change. People involved in any group need to be happy not only with themselves, they need to be happy with others in the group and with the progress of the group.

Last evening I attended a council meeting for a local community school. Since this was the first meeting for the new council members, each one introduced himself and explained what he was doing in life. I was surprised to see that an acquaintance of mine was a member of this council. This man is a part of a Christian group to which I belong. Frankly, I am a bit embarrassed by his appearance and by his trite conversation. When it was his turn to explain what he does in life, I was relieved when he did not mention the Christian group to which we both belong. (Maybe *he* was embarrassed that *I* belonged to that group and he did not want to be identified with me either.) But probably if he and I knew one another better, we would appreciate each other's gifts and abilities and the unity would be maximized between us.

A Time-Life televison program about fish recently demonstrated the difference between an aggregate of fish and a school of fish. The difference is that an aggregate has no coordinated movement. Surely there is a difference between Christians who merely meet in the same place on Sunday and a body of believers who move together in a coordinated fashion. Unity requires relationship. It also requires compromise (see chapter 5) on the part of all of those involved in the group.

Reasons for Disunity.
"I assumed I was supposed to be at the meeting and get someone else to take my speaking engagement." "And *I* assumed that, since you had a speaking engagement, you would fulfill that responsibility and not be able to attend our meeting." This difference resulted one week when our church governing board

changed its meeting from Thursday morning to Wednesday night. The board chairman assumed that one staff member would not attend the meeting since he was scheduled to lead a Bible study. The staff member assumed that he should get a replacement for his engagement and attend the meeting. We saw a bit of confusion and some damaged feelings until the matter was openly discussed. In a church setting, one should never assume that all those involved have the same understanding of the goals of the group. There must be communication on what you think ought to be done. So often, disunity results from a lack of communication.

"Who is Mrs. Cole?" asked one of our new board members. That question is almost unbelievable in our church. Mrs. Cole is one of the stalwarts of the faith. She did all the volunteer secretarial work before I came to the church, and for some time afterwards. She was the church's first paid secretary, and she has been working in that capacity for a number of years. It is difficult to accept the fact that someone as involved as a board member and someone else as involved as a church secretary had never met. That the church people know one another (or even each other's names) should never be assumed. It is always my practice to introduce people to one another when we are standing in a group talking. Often, of course, they already know each other. But often they do not. I'm sure I carry this practice to an extreme. One day I'll probably try to introduce a husband and wife to one another. But in a city with high mobility, I see great need for people to become initially acquainted and then to spend time together so that they can know one another's hearts and move together in unity.

"What do you mean, no commercial kitchen?" one of our staff members stormed. Having worked for many months on the building committee, he assumed that everyone was in agreement concerning the kitchen. The plans had been drawn to accommodate a commercial kitchen. Yet when it came time to simply ratify that decision, several of the building committee members admitted they had never heard that a commercial kitchen was in the planning. They had assumed that a small domestic kitchen was all that was going to be necessary in the new building. Again, it was a mistake to assume that people knew and understood the same facts.

The effective leader who wants to create orderly change from within the church will propagate unity. But remember that there is a difference between a boss and a leader.

BOSS	LEADER
drives	coaches
depends on authority	depends on good will
inspires fear	inspires enthusiasm
says "I"	says "We"
assigns the task	sets the pace
says "be on time"	beats everyone there
fixes the blame	fixes the breakdown

The leader promotes unity; the boss does not. Walt Henrichsen, in his book *Disciples Are Made Not Born*, says, "The mark of leadership is servanthood. Chesty Puller, considered by many as Mr. Marine, stated once that the Marine Corps needed men who could lead, not command. A commander tells people what to do; a leader shows people what to do by personal example."[23]

A couple of years ago, I took a river trip by rubber raft, starting in Colorado and ending in Utah. During the course of the several days' journey, each person in each of the rafts had the opportunity to be the leader of his particular raft. As we approached each set of rapids, each leader would tell all of us how to paddle to get through that set of rapids. Sometimes the leader became frustrated or excited. When he did, he gave poor instructions. So we all had to face the issue of how to follow our leaders. We knew that if we did what some of those leaders told us, we would suddenly flip the raft and tumble into the water.

Most Christians are aware of the importance of unity, and yet inevitably they face the question of how far to follow a leader. Following a leader involves not only unity but sometimes the priorities of common sense or even morals and ethics.

Peter Moreno was the junior department superintendent. LeRoy Stevens, the Sunday school superintendent, wanted to institute a Sunday school contest in Peter's department, to create interest and build attendance. Peter thought the goals were worthy, but he did not agree with the method. He felt that a Sunday school contest would not produce the results any of them wanted. In this case, he had to make a choice between unity and his personal beliefs.

"I'll just photocopy enough copies for everyone in the choir. That way we won't have to buy a book for each person." That phrase has probably been heard many times in Christian circles. Many believers have been dishonest with publishing firms in the matter of copying music. The publishing houses make it clear that it is dishonest to reproduce music in such a fashion. Yet what should one do when a mature Christian makes such a suggestion? Is it too harsh to explain that the practice is dishonest and that such a procedure must not be followed? In Colorado Springs we face a further dilemma when military personnel volunteer to buy something for the church (for which they will be reimbursed) at the subsidized price from the military commissary. Government rules clearly state that such a practice is illegal. The one making the offer is doing so in order to save the church money, but he can do so only by breaking a law. Here again we see that unity is not the only matter under consideration. Many times moral or ethical considerations will hinder change or derail unity. But that is the risk we must take when we operate on the premise that God is in control and that we are to obey the Word of God in all things.

"Your silence frightens me," I said after a particularly controversial sermon. I was asking for feedback (as I do each Sunday) —and there was none. My immediate reaction was that either the congregation fully agreed with me and accepted what I had said in the message, or they did not agree at all and the silence was an indication of their disapproval. Unity is important to leaders who wish to create change. But don't let yourself think you have unity just because you feel no flak. Maybe everyone is unified simply in doing nothing. Or maybe the lack of verbal disagreement is a boycott of your ideas. Always evaluate the calm. It may be the still that precedes a storm.

"Why can't Jack Sparks teach in this church anymore?" This question came from several different, sincere people who wondered why their friend was suddenly being blacklisted in the church. The truth was that there was no blacklist at all. Rather, Jack was going to be traveling a great deal during the coming quarter, and the committee making teaching assignments felt it was best that he not teach during that period of frequent absence. Somehow the concept of not teaching got twisted to mean "not allowed to teach." Simple communication of information can make a lot of difference in the unity of a church. Sometimes two conflicting parties may have been exposed to different information and thus have arrived at a different understanding of the issues and what course of action would make the most sense. Often the mere lack of information causes disunity. In one church when a new missions committee was created, the ladies who had been active in the ladies' missionary group naturally assumed that their organization was going to be discontinued. That certainly was not the case. The truth was that the leaders had outlined distinct purposes, priorities, and ministries for each group, but had not clearly communicated to the ladies what their relationship to the new missions committee would be.

How often has it happened in a church that the new youth minister suddenly faces a mass resignation from everyone working with the young people? The workers have assumed that hiring a new youth minister means that he will do all the work. Again someone has created disunity by not distributing proper information.

"I thought you had appointed someone else to do my job," a lady of our church told me. She was on a deaconess committee and her job was that of hospitality. Separately from her job, we had arranged to have someone in charge of special meals and refreshments for new visitors to the church. The deaconess' job had to do with hospitality for those who were already members of the church. Her job was to organize and direct the after-church fellowship for the entire body. The new program needed a new person and system. Yet we had failed to communicate to those involved with the older and ongoing system that the new system would not affect them in any way.

The chairman of the music committee approached the church organist and asked how much he was spending on the purchase of organ music. The organist immediately recoiled and thought, "What business does he have to ask me that?" The fact was that the organist graciously bought all of his own music that he played in the church. He was happy with that arrangement. He liked to build his own library with new pieces of music. The music committee chairman was asking so that he could suggest that the music committee put into next year's budget sufficient money to purchase organ music. He felt that he was doing the organist a favor. The two people had a perceptional difference about the issue before them.

Many times a difference in perception causes disunity and creates an atmosphere that hinders change in the church. On another occasion, the pastor of a beginning church was asked to complete a progress report on the new church he was leading. It had been born just six months earlier, and the sponsoring church wanted some facts and figures to help them evaluate what was happening in the daughter church. When the new pastor was asked to complete the form, he perceived that the motive was to fire him because of displeasure. The administration of the sponsoring church had no such idea at all.

One church board member perceives that his responsibility is to make decisions that affect the church. Another member of the same board perceives that his responsibility is only to rubber-stamp what the church staff brings to the board. It is quite necessary to understand how people perceive their roles and what they think they ought to be doing in each particular ministry. Regardless of what the organizational chart shows, some pastors believe they are in charge of the board. Other pastors believe that the board is in charge of the church staff. Regardless of which approach is accepted in a local congregation (of course both sides appeal to the Scriptures to justify their positions), it is necessary that all people in one church have the same perception of who has authority over whom. It really doesn't matter if the Sunday school teacher is given complete control over the content that is delivered in his class or if the Christian education board is charged with the responsibility of selecting and coordinating all of the curriculum. What matters is that the body will suffer disunity and conflict if the Sunday school teacher has one perception and the Christian education board has another.

Some church staff members feel that every man should work independently, each person doing his own ministry without consulting the other. Other people on that same church staff may have the idea that the whole point of a church staff is for the members of the team to spend a great deal of time planning together. Again, there may be no right or wrong, but the same perception must be shared by all. If a church usher perceives that his role is only to pass the offering plates, he may come into conflict with church board members who believe the usher should be alert for new ways to make the auditorium more comfortable.

Written job descriptions for every position in the church will help eliminate problems caused by perceptual differences. If the Sunday school teacher receives a job description before he begins his task, he will know who is responsible for his curriculum. He will understand the authority structure and more than likely will have less trouble and conflict in his new position. Job descriptions need to be available at all times. A church without job descriptions can begin by asking each person in a place of responsibility to write his own. You can provide a simple format so that the form of all job descriptions is fairly consistent.

One-page job descriptions are probably the best. At the top of the page write: "JOB DESCRIPTION FOR _____." Then a short paragraph explaining each of the following is adequate: qualification for this position, duties of this position, responsible for, responsible to.

Probably every church treasurer has been faced with the temptation of restricting funds from the church budget. Normally the structure of churches is that the treasurer only writes checks, while someone else is responsible for making the decisions to pay. But sometimes church treasurers become impressed with their own authority and begin to make decisions about the money rather than simply writing the check to issue the money.

Sometimes the newly elected member of a board or committee will create disunity because he is impressed with his new-found authority. This evil slips into the hearts of Christians without their even recognizing what has happened. When people become resistant to their authority, and conflicts arise, the one who has been impressed with his own authority often reacts by draping himself in robes of righteousness, while viewing those who oppose him as ugly creatures stirring up trouble.

In First Church, one Sunday school class is composed of older adults who have been together for decades. That class, quite large, wields a great deal of power in the total structure. The teacher, who has become a permanent fixture, has built himself a kingdom that he is not about to allow to be decentralized. Whenever an issue comes up in the church, this adult class, led by its teacher, can swing the vote one way or the other.

Kingdom-building can also create disunity when a youth director or teacher builds a personal kingdom with his proteges. The young people can become a mighty force for good or ill in any church. Kingdom-building can take place with any Sunday school teacher, club leader or committee chairman. Wherever a kingdom builder has selfishly thought only of his own sphere rather than of the total ministry, there will be disunity. The sin of kingdom-building is just that: selfishness, thinking only of one's own ministry rather than the total ministry of the body of Christ in any local setting.

I know a fine church with a long and outstanding history that is actually run by a church secretary. This dear woman was the senior minister's secretary for many years. The senior pastor did not enjoy administration, so he placed a great deal of authority and responsibility upon the shoulders of his secretary. She actually developed into an administrative assistant, although her title was always that of secretary. When the senior minister retired after many distinguished years of service, the secretary stayed in her position and built walls around her own kingdom. The principal of the day school which operated in that particular church even had to go to the secretary to ask to turn on the heat each fall and the air-conditioning each spring. He could not use the gymnasium without the approval of the church secretary. She loved her authority and frequently would not give permission for such elementary matters, although the church board approved all such mechanical functions. Her kingdom became so strong that not even the church board dared to rebuke her. When candidates for the pastorate of that church sensed the situation they quit pursuing the relationship.

Sooner or later disunity results from such domination by any member of the body. Disunity comes because people start with different assumptions, information, perceptions. Sometimes disunity creeps in through selfishness.

Disagreement vs. Disunity.
"It is because of dumb meetings like that that we need to make those changes." Those words were spoken in anger to me after a church business meeting. The church leaders had tried to take a step toward a board-run church. Our proposal was that all of the officers and committees be appointed by the governing board rather than through the mechanism of elections. The process of election had become no more than a popularity contest and, because of the size of the church, we could never hope that the matter would improve. It seemed logical and right to take this step. The congregation, however, wanted to retain some final authority. They amended the motion to read that the congregation would have final ratification authority.

In reality, this was similar to what was going on anyway. But on the other hand, we had moved a step closer to our original proposal. To my colleague who was a bit bothered by the amendment which passed, I commented, "It seems as though we will have to accept what we got tonight and believe that it is God's will for this time, and be happy that we moved one step closer to our original intention. One day we will have the full authority on the board to make those changes without going through some of these time-wasting motions."

Stupid. Resistant. Stiffnecked. Traditional. Conservative. These and other such terms are often hurled in anger by those who want to create change within the church. Seeing that other people in the church do not want change, they judge the motives and credibility of those who will not cooperate with their new ideas. But the one wishing to create change within the church should remember another word which describes people who resist change. That word is *normal*. When the one wishing to create a change makes that discovery, he will change his own attitude. Then usually he will notice that his proposals for change are accepted more readily in the body.

Please do not keep a pious look on your face about the preceding paragraph. You too, no matter how progressive and change-oriented you are, will resist some changes when they are initially presented to you. I can think of many times when I have resisted, though later I have become a change agent to institute those very same matters. That does not mean that the one who resists change and later accepts the exact change that was formerly offered is being inconsistent. It means that a normal progression for most people is first to resist. Remember that it is better not to create a change if that will create disunity. Take half of the pie (see chapter 5) and be happy with that change. Then come back later for the rest of the dessert.

Now of course, it may be true that some of the epitaphs about the still-living people in your church are true. Nonetheless, accept it as a challenge to change those who seem least likely to change. I still remember vividly the traditional situation into which I walked in my present pastorate. On my first Sunday in the church

I was the only man in the congregation not wearing a white dress shirt. Now I smile inside when I see some of those formerly very traditional men today wearing beautiful pastel shirts and growing mustaches and beards.

"We need to change that system," recommended a new member of the board. "No, we can't do that. We have already tried and it cannot be changed," remarked a long-time member of the board. "Well, it can be changed and it should be," responded the new man. In less than sixty seconds the change was instituted.

When the chairman of the board turned to me and said "Motion carried," I was still sitting in shock. Never had I seen the board steamroll that long-time member in such fashion. The older member is a wonderful Christian, and he has been on the board for many years; yet it suddenly became apparent that there was a new dynamic on the board. The new man did not have respect for the older member's past contributions. He simply saw that a change needed to be made, and the proposal got the necessary votes. The beautiful part of the story is that the disagreement did not cause disunity. Sometimes those who want to create change fear that any disagreement causes disunity. But that certainly is not true.

Some churches have the rule that their official board will not act without a unanimous decision on all matters. I now serve on a board that formerly adhered to that policy. As long as I have been on that certain board, which is not associated with our church, we have made only one decision that was not unanimous. In that particular situation we needed to change personnel. Four of the five of us believed that the change needed to take place. The fifth man, who was very close to the person under consideration, thought there was still a chance of redeeming this person and allowing her to keep her job. We put off the decision for three months. We prayed. We collected more data, and we met. It was a stalemate. Finally, as chairman of the board, I called for a vote, and it was four to one. I believe that it is unwise to require that all decisions of a board or committee always be unanimous. To make such a requirement assumes that all members are always able to set aside all of their prejudices, backgrounds, and dynamics of their old natures on all issues. That is a heavy assumption.

People sometimes vote for or against a proposition, not according to their convictions, but according to their wish not to create disunity among the members. That motive hardly lends credibility to the requirement of unanimity on all issues. Furthermore, the requirement of unanimity slows down change more than is necessary. The simple truth is that disagreement need not cause disunity. Christians ought to be able to face one another lovingly and peaceably on issues concerning which they honestly and openly disagree. Speak the truth in love as you understand it, and vote that way if necessary. That process need not cause unkindness, hostility or alienation.

The Clarks and the Gonzaleses co-sponsor the youth group at their church. When both couples assumed that responsibility, the young people always met at 6:00 P.M. on Sundays to sing and to listen to a lesson taught by one of the adults. This youth meeting was fairly well attended. The kids sang and listened each Sunday for an hour before the Sunday evening service. One evening when song requests were being made, someone suggested a nonreligious song. The group cheered its approval and sang it. The kids then suggested several other nonreligious songs, and the evening was off in a new direction.

After the evening service the Gonzaleses invited the Clarks into their home. After hanging their coats in the hall closet Dave Gonzales exploded to the Clarks: "Wasn't that a disgrace in the youth meeting? Those are the kinds of songs unsaved kids sing. Don't our young people know they are different? Christians should not try to copy the world!" Well, the Clarks were astonished at the Gonzaleses' reaction. They didn't know what to say. They thought the different songs were terrific. There was an enthusiasm in the singing that they had never witnessed prior to that evening.

The Clarks wisely tried to present their position in a low-key manner. No doubt about it, there was a sharp disagreement between the two couples sponsoring the youth group. Yet in this case disagreement did not cause disunity. In fact, the tension served as a trampoline from which to bounce creative ideas into the air. As alternatives became visible, a new attitude developed. Neither couple were defensive about their views. Both couples were willing to see the options as they bounced from the lips of all four of the leaders. After further discussion among themselves and with the young people it was decided to scrap the whole concept of singing at the Sunday evening youth meeting. Surprisingly the sponsors learned that the group really was tired of singing and that even the new songs weren't really important to them. As the sponsors entered into deeper dialogue, more changes took place. They changed the meeting time to after the evening service. Games and food replaced singing. Sharing and teen prayers replaced the lessons taught by adults.

All of the changes were received enthusiastically by the young people, the church leaders, and the parents. But those changes might have never been born without an initial disagreement. Don't see disagreement as evil. Look at it as an opportunity to search for creative alternatives that might not have been forced upon you otherwise.

Disagreement often forces deeper and more serious consideration of our approaches and programs. Don't immediately defend your current circumstances and ministries. Maybe there is a better way. Listen to the complainer. He may be your best friend! Too often we settle for mediocre ministries just because no one is outspokenly unhappy.

But suppose that either the Gonzaleses or the Clarks had allowed the disagreement to deteriorate into disunity. How does one handle conflict so that it doesn't go the wrong direction? Squashing disagreement doesn't always help. That may only create more conflict. The whole idea of freedom (chapter one) dictates that we establish some creative ways to handle conflicts. Conflict is normal. Expect it. But learn to handle it properly.

1. *Keep the channels open.* Robert was again disrupting the youth meeting. This time it was during prayer. And this was the brick

that broke the laborer's back. "Out," I demanded. "Leave, go away, and never return." As the sponsor for the youth group, I exercised my "right" to remove the troublemaker. After the meeting I learned that Robert's parents had vowed to nail me to the church steeple. They were taking me to the highest court in that church—the pastor. So I quickly gathered my own forces. Without much difficulty I rounded up five adults who were willing to testify that in the last several years they had quit teaching certain youth groups or Sunday school classes because Robert had made their ministry so miserable.

When showdown time came, I was ready. Robert's parents sat with their darling son on the blue sofa at one side of the pastor's study. I sat in the metal folding chair on the other side of the office. We each presented our cases. I clearly won, I thought. I expected never to see Robert again. Surely this wise pastor we all loved and respected would agree with me and never allow that brat back into my meeting.

But alas, the pastor split his vote. He reprimanded Robert for his behavior. He admonished the parents to uphold authority. And Robert could return to the meeting next week! I was furious!!! After Robert and his parents left, I stayed to talk with the pastor. "You made a mistake," I blurted out. "I know you are older and you are the pastor . . ." "And don't you forget that, Mike," the pastor interrupted with raised eyebrows and a stern voice.

That whole series of events is an ugly example of how not to handle conflict. Doors were slamming in every room. No hallway was opened. I had not left a channel open for Robert or his parents. They had left no alternatives for me. Even the pastor who made a wise decision slammed a door in my face with his harsh authoritarian reminder of his control.

When conflicts arise, remember to back off and consciously work at keeping the channels open. See the positive options available. Don't dig in. Remain flexible. Such a position will encourage your opponent to loosen up also, so that meaningful exchange can transpire and the conflict can be creatively resolved to further the objectives of all parties.

2. *Talk about* what *is right, not* who *is right*. Harry thought the church should purchase the house next door and remodel it for use as additional Sunday school space. Bill opposed the idea. He said the church couldn't afford the remodeling costs now, and besides, it would not really meet their needs anyway. They needed room for their growing college class as well as room for the juniors and junior high students. As the weeks rolled along, Harry and Bill each dug in and lobbied for support for his own views. Soon the whole board was taking sides. Every member was either on Bill's or Harry's side. The chairman then wisely suggested that the decision must be based on what is right, not who is right. That suggestion removed the tumor of trouble that was growing. Depersonalizing decisions makes them less emotional and usually raises the probability that they will be right decisions.

In this particular case the board decided to purchase the house but not remodel it. The juniors could use it as it was. The junior high department moved into the space occupied by the college class. And that class moved across the street to meet in a restaurant. Several years later when the church built additional educational space, the house was sold at a profit. Everyone was happy and Bill and Harry are still friends.

3. *See the other's frame of reference*. Several people in the church had complained about Doug. He was really obnoxious: loud, crude, and rude. He could offend more people in five minutes than most Christians do in five years. Some people actually turned and walked the other way when they saw Doug approaching. Then one night during a sharing time Doug explained his struggles. He admitted that he had lots of rough edges. He asked the Body to pray for him as he worked on his problems. During his talk he explained a bit about how it was in his life before his conversion to Christ several years ago. What a difference that testimony made in people's attitudes! Now they no longer look

merely at where Doug is or isn't. They see where he is in reference to where he once was.

When conflict arises, take time to see the other person's background and his present context of life. Maybe you would react the way Joe did if you were under the pressures he lives with each day. If you were laden with the fears that Mary carries deep inside, you might act irresponsibly too. And dear Mrs. Stubbins was raised in another era.

4. *Don't judge motives*. "I believe you are a godly man who sincerely believes you are acting on God's orders." The man who said that to me this week is a man with whom I have a serious conflict. For several weeks we have been talking and praying together, trying to either resolve our differences or decide to go separate ways. He has graciously given me the benefit of not judging my motives. We are really clashing on some rather major issues, but there is a good hope that we can resolve the problem. Call your opponent stupid or lazy or uninformed if you must, but don't judge his motives. Once you allow yourself to believe that your opposition is acting or believing the way he is because he is greedy or power-hungry or selfish, the conflict has little chance of being resolved in a happy way. If you do honestly believe that the other party has an evil motive, confront him and say so. Don't accuse, but simply say, "Pete, it appears to me that your motive for wanting this change is a selfish one. I'm not saying it is, only that it frankly appears to me that way. Please straighten me out on that." This approach will force the other individual to either admit his error (at least in part) or defend himself without being defensive since you asked for an explanation. This kind of confrontation can often break the log-jam to allow the stream of communication to flow again.

5. *Be open to meaningful participation by all*. The lady who carefully grooms her hair but rarely bathes is not caring for her body properly. A beautiful hairdo will not compensate for body odor! All parts of the body need to be recognized as significant. That is true physically and spiritually with the Body of Christ. Each Christian in the church needs meaningful opportunity to express

himself when he is involved in conflict. Maybe the pastor is wrong and the janitor is right about the schedule for cleaning. Perhaps the ten-year-old has a legitimate complaint about the way the Brigade program operates.

6. *Look for short-term or intermediate goals.* When the building committee started planning for the new church facility, sharp disagreement arose. Jerry insisted that a gymnasium was needed as a first unit. It could be used for recreation and for worship. Frank opposed the plan. He expressed his opinion that the church buildings should be built for worship, not for recreation. As the two men handled their conflict and worked together for a mutually agreeable solution, they centered on the principles listed here. Their conclusion was that the first unit would include an auditorium for worship. The second unit, to be built in five years, would include a gym. In the meantime they agreed to rent a nearby public school gym each Wednesday night for recreation.

Our conflicts make us aware of where we differ with others. But we need to remember where we *agree* with those same people. Frank really wasn't so opposed to the idea of a gym. He really opposed the gym only because to build it as a first unit would mean that an appropriate auditorium would have to wait. So the two men learned to focus on their agreements and thus have a base on which to establish some short-term, long-term, and intermediate goals.

7. *Build mutual trust.* "She's on the phone four hours a day gathering her friends into her camp." How often have small conflicts in a church been ballooned completely out of proportion because someone created an "us and them" attitude? Have you ever listened carefully to friends talk about mutual opponents and refer to the other side as "them"? That's deadly. When Christians choose up sides, both sides lose! Mutual trust is built by refusing to gather forces for yourself in opposition to "them."

Of course, it may be that you do need to inform others and solicit their help. But be honest with your opposition. Give others the benefit of the doubt when you hear that they've said a nasty thing about you. Keep the fight clean. Uphold your view in such a way that those who oppose you will say that you are fair. This principle summarizes and results from the previous six.

In the church we cannot avoid conflict, and we should not want to. It has advantages. But wholesome conflict does not legislate for disunity or against change.

Symbolisms and Festivals to Encourage Unity.

In a well-known dramatic role, actor Zero Mostel says that it is very hard for people to exist in his little village of Anatevka. So why do people stay there? Because that is their home. How do they keep their balance? By tradition. The faraway village of Anatevka holds many traditions. There is the tradition of wearing a small head covering. How did the tradition get started? No one knows. But it is a tradition; and traditions, sings Mostel, help the people to know how to live and to understand what God wants them to do. At the end of the song from the well-known play and movie, the star says that without traditions the people would be as shaky as . . . well, as a fiddler on the roof.

When Nancy and I were first wed we wanted to throw out all family traditions. We saw no value in keeping or creating traditions in our new family. It was not long, however, before we realized that we had made a mistake. There is value in tradition. It makes life fun. We enjoy the anticipation of the forthcoming practice of traditions. In addition to the regular Thanksgiving, Christmas, and other holiday traditions, we enjoy taking a short trip during "spring break." Since our church has only one service on Easter Sunday, we usually do something special on that evening. And on birthdays we have the tradition that the birthday person has his choice of food for the evening meal. When we are camping our tradition is that the one starting the campfire must do it with only one match and no paper.

God's people in the Old Testament were full of traditions. The entire sacrificial system was traditional and symbolic. The way the people dressed spoke of a deeper meaning. The Israelites frequently erected altars or towers to remind them of past events. It is clearly stated in Scripture that rocks were piled on one another so that when the children would ask about them the adults would be able to remind the children of God's hand upon the nation in that particular circumstance. Tradition and symbolism were important in the Old Testament. The New Testament also encourages symbolisms, festivals, and traditions. Baptism has historically been the symbol of a spiritual birth. The Lord's Supper is a symbol and festival of that which has happened in the past.

Symbolisms, festivals, and traditions are really what the psychologists call "acting out." Acting out is an important part of a healthy life. That is why we have graduation ceremonies and marriage ceremonies. And after a death, a funeral service helps the bereaved express grief over the loss of a loved one. In a festival people can act as they are expected to act. No explanation is necessary for people crying or laughing at appropriate times. Most festivals also have a special musical form attached to them. Often there is a special form of parade. Edgar Jackson explains the psychological significance of such events:

Ceremonial acting out meets the needs of the total person—the mind, the emotions and the body are all involved. The meaning of the event speaks to a person's mental needs and the language of ceremony often carries deep insight that nourishes the mind. At the same time it provides an atmosphere where deep feelings will be at home.[24]

Our culture's emphasis on objective truth may have caused us to grow to neglect subjective truth. Both are necessary. Our emphasis on objective truth may have taken some of the beauty out of Christianity. In some places our faith has been molded into a cold, stony set of propositions. Of course, the evangelical Christian believes in objective, propositional truth. That does not necessitate that we neglect the rest of our nature. Doctrine is important, but so is beauty. Some Christians grump about rock-and-roll music, yet their form of country gospel is not one ounce musically superior.

And look at our church buildings—boxes and rectangles. We have overreacted against Gothic cathedrals. It *is* repulsive to see the huge and expensive churches in Italy while next door the people who attend that church live in hovels with cardboard walls. Yet, God still loves beauty. How pleasant it is to see some churches today building with beauty and landscaping in mind. The present emphasis on ecology and environment make it necessary that churches carefully plan their buildings and building sites. It may be that we have reacted so far that our churches have no symbol of the faith. Have we gone too far?

If Christians can attend the local symphony and enjoy beautiful music, why can't we use that same beauty in our churches? There is a place for gospel songs. But isn't there also a place for Brahms? Do not symbols created by lovely music—Christian or not—bring us closer to God and to all that he created?

It is possible that we have worked so diligently at negating the Roman Catholic emphasis on the Lord's Supper that we have stripped the symbol of its meaning? Protestants do not believe that the elements are actually the blood and body of Christ. That is good theology. But we must resist the temptation to crudely refer to the elements as crackers and grape juice. Some churches insist that the whole act be called an ordinance rather than a sacrament. This is usually done to emphasize that no grace is imparted through the observance. But is there grace imparted? Most of us agree that the observance does not deliver inherent value. But when we take the elements and remember the meaning attached to them, that does deliver a value to our lives. Can that—even loosely—be called the impartation of grace? Perhaps Protestants, especially evangelicals, need to rethink the eucharist.

Certainly there is a danger that people will substitute the symbol for the reality, but there is also the danger that without the proper balance the symbol is meaningless. Jesus instructed the church to observe the Supper until his return. Some churches interpret that to mean that the observance is to be done each week. Others feel that once a month or once a quarter is sufficient. The frequency is not the issue. The point is the meaning. The New Testament does instruct Christians in symbols and traditions. Historically we have forgotten that truth.

Scores of people have come to me and given testimony that

their baptism was a significant step forward in their Christian lives. I often tell people that I do not understand why such a simple act can be so very meaningful. But it is. I am positive that it helps people in their walk with Jesus Christ. It is a simple act that takes only a few moments, but I always tell candidates for baptism that they will look back upon the day of their baptism as a significant step forward in their lives. It is encouraging to see that many Christians of all denominations are realizing that baptism is a symbolic act which should be observed by the individual after he has willingly entered into a new relationship with Jesus Christ. Even churches which historically practice infant baptism are now offering adult baptism for those who wish to participate.

Most Christians believe that baptism is only a symbol of deeper inward change. But the challenge is that we be careful not to rip away the beauty of the act. Symbols do create unity. When the Body of Christ meets and observes the Lord's Table there is a unifying factor in that act. And when the church gathers and observes believers identifying with the Body through the act of baptism, that too is a unifying factor. The one wishing to create change in the church should realize that these timeless symbolic acts established by God can be used (not manipulated) to help create meaningful and wholesome change for the Body.

In Old Testament times, God's people had feasts several times a year. Those events helped to weld the people into a unity. A typical church of today experiences few such events. In some churches the annual missions conference, evangelistic meetings, or prophetic conference may be as close as they get to a festival. In other churches the choir's Christmas cantata or the vacation Bible school may be seen as annual highlights.

But most of those happenings are work- and ministry-oriented meetings. Surely there is no problem with that, but in addition there is the need to have a festival for fun in the church. Annual trips and meals together can be a unifying factor in any group. The old-fashioned "dinner on the ground" that southern churches once enjoyed helped those churches to come together in unity and harmony.

Celebration is powerful. The leaders wanting to create change in a church may discover that a potluck meal once a quarter yields more of an opportunity to talk about and create change than all the board and business meetings of an entire year!

Many evangelicals rebel at the historical preaching calendar observed in liturgical denominations. Almost every Sunday has a particular meaning according to church history. Yet even those who do not wish to follow such a form may find value in setting apart certain Sundays to remember events of church history or to recall events of that particular local congregation. It would be a unifying event to annually remember church members who have gone to be with the Lord. Events that celebrate the paying off of the mortgage or the groundbreaking of a new building always bring the people closer together. In times of happiness and festivity the change agent will discover that the group is more ready to receive an additional challenge for change.

On the Sunday we wanted to present the proposal for erecting a $1.25 million building the leaders needed the church's permission to hire an architect, enter into a contract with a builder, and sell the present buildings. That is a great deal to care for in one meeting. For that event we canceled our evening service and had a grand meal together following the morning service. The whole event took place on the ranch of one of the people of the church. During the afternoon there was plenty of recreation. After a good meal and lots of fun together we met and discussed the proposal. All of the motions passed. Looking back upon that event we feel that certainly one of the factors was that we were having fun together and our hearts were knit in unity before the business was transacted. It was a good setting for the introduction of change.

"We have organized the truth more than God did." That statement at first startled me. Then I realized that it is true. Certainly there is a place for systematically studying the Bible according to topics. Systematic theology is a valid and legitimate discipline. Yet it may be that such study has created a "theologizing" of our faith. Perhaps we have created systems that separate us from one another. As you scrutinize the pages of twentieth century church history you will notice that the divisions among demoninations and churches in this century were usually not due to major doctrinal differences. Rather, Christians have argued about minor differences. Churches have often divided over issues of personalities and emphases rather than basic doctrine. How Satan must smile when he accomplishes divisions among Christians.

Recently a member of our pastoral staff presented the idea for a new church brochure. On the first page was a brief summary of our doctrine. That's awful! What nonchurch person (or even most church members) would take time to read our doctrinal statement? Yet when you open the first page of any Christian school catalog there it is—the doctrinal statement. Church constitutions usually begin by naming the corporation, listing the church covenant, and filling pages telling you about their doctrine.

Now it must be clear that I am not against written doctrinal statements. I have written quite a few for churches and for Christian organizations. It is good and proper for an individual or an organization to state its beliefs. But that approach is part of the problem. We present our faith as a set of beliefs rather than as a life. We insist that new members in our churches subscribe to our doctrinal statements. Yet we never seem to get around to asking the prospective member if he gossips, if he is honest in his business, or whether or not he is involved in serving other people to demonstrate the love of Christ.

Our emphasis on specialized creeds needs to be changed. Frankly, I believe it is a great cause for disunity in our churches. It has a deadening effect on change. We waste much time nit-picking nonessentials rather than emphasizing changed lives. There really is not much difference in the way those who hold a pretribulational view of the rapture and those who hold a posttribulational view live their lives! When will we learn that nonessential matters should not be a test of spirituality, fellowship, or cooperation? I have suggested to our church that we express only the essential doctrines in our church constitution. I see no need whatsoever to state in a constitution any other doctrines than those that we believe the Bible teaches about God, man, and salvation. Certainly there are times when we should state other points of our belief also, but those can be shown in a set of bylaws or in a policy book. It is not necessary for a person to understand and believe exactly as the founding fathers of our church believed in all areas before he can fellowship, worship, and serve God in our church.

By the way, have you ever noticed the kinds of things a doctrinal statement includes? Since one cannot usually put down *all* that he believes about the Bible's teaching, he has to make choices. The choices come in two categories: what is important and what is his current hobby or reaction. That's right. People put in doctrinal statements what they believe is essential plus what they happen to be upset about at the time they write the statement. My suggestion is that Christian organizations and churches work at deleting the hobbies and reactions, so as to focus on the major issues. That will help create unity in the church and that will expedite change for the glory of the Lord.

Four
ORGANIZE
PROPERLY

Pastor Vinton hardly blinked anymore. The wide-eyed young pastor was rejoicing at the new growth his church was experiencing. He was so excited about leading his church into new areas of ministry that he feared missing another blessing that might come his way. Since he started serving the North Side Bible Church only nine months earlier, it had leaped from 75 to 136 average Sunday morning attendance. Never had the church experienced a growth pattern of that proportion. Chaplain Monsen, an elder in the church, who was in fact responsible for the church's contact with Pastor Vinton, was on active duty in the military, but his present assignment allowed him freedom to participate in the local church. Vinton considered himself fortunate to have an older, wiser minister to be his mentor. Frequently the two sat at lunch while the pastor pried open the mind of the chaplain. "Chaplain, how long will this growth at North Side last? Can we expect a continued increase?" "Only," warned the senior man, "if you are wise enough to delegate and manage well."

Delegate? Manage? Those are terms of the world! In the church we should talk about the Word, spiritual growth, conversions, baptism, ministries. Most church leaders don't have time to manage. They want to minister. And that is the problem! Most church leaders see management as an enemy of ministry. They need to understand that proper management *is* ministry, and that any effective ministry must have management to sustain and perpetuate it.

Management is simply getting things done through people. Why can't the "things" of the last sentence be ministry? Some Christians have done so well at neglecting organization and management that they are effectively limiting their own ministries. They want change in their church, but they can't see the need for systems and good management because they drape "God-words" over the whole church. "The New Testament church wasn't highly organized, and we don't need to be either." "We just let the Lord run our church." "Just preach the gospel and everything else will fall into place." "As long as we give to missions, that's all that matters." Many churches hide their failures with "spiritual" clichés. These Christians sincerely do want to see more people reached, more given to missions, a better Sunday school; but it has never occurred to them that they just are not properly organized to do the job.

Of course, it is true that a well-oiled machine acting as a church will not necessarily do spiritual ministry. It is possible to have a highly efficient organization that lacks spiritual direction, purpose, and power. I admit that a church can be properly organized and not spiritual, but I insist that a church can't be spiritual without being properly organized. It is wrong for church leaders to neglect the duty of management. Without proper management and organization even the most spiritual group of Christians who live together in a local church will remain small and ineffective. The first church in Jerusalem soon discovered this need in the Body (Acts 6). They tried several systems in order to do the best job possible in their context. When Paul established churches he appointed leaders (Acts 14:23). Leaders were trained (Barnabas, Timothy, Luke, and others). And a performance evaluation standard was constructed (1 Timothy 3:1-13).

Management is different from leadership. Engstrom makes the distinction:

It is important to distinguish between management and leadership. In essence, leadership is a broader concept than management. Management is thought of as a social kind of leadership in which the accomplishment of organizational goals is paramount. While leadership also involves working with and through people to accomplish goals, these are not necessarily organizational goals.[25]

Leadership involves helping Henry be a better employee, husband, and father. Management is limited to helping Henry be a better Sunday school teacher. Both are important. Both are spiritual. The larger the church, and the higher the individual is in the hierarchy of that church, the more management work he is required to do. To neglect management work is to neglect a large part of what God has called every leader to do.

While attending school working for a doctorate, I traveled

home on weekends. On one particular weekend we had class on Saturday, so when I arrived at the church office on Sunday my desk was buried under piles of paper. During one of the Sunday morning services (I had already attended one service) I rolled up my sleeves and dug into the work—mail, notes, decisions, memos. Then I heard it, "Pastor, do you have a minute to talk?" Mike, president of the singles group and a very likable fellow, was standing in my doorway. I love this brother and would greatly enjoy spending much more time with him. Mike is even planning to attend the seminary from which I graduated. But you see the tension—management work or personal conversation and counseling.

In such a situation some leaders piously proclaim that people always come first. But the truth was that if I could not answer those memos, make those decisions, and respond to that correspondence, I would be violating the trust other *people* had placed in me. Those pieces of paper on my desk represented people as much as that body in my doorway. The decision was not between people and things, but between people and people. Now this is very important. Some leaders are always available to people who show up at the door, to the detriment of getting management work done. That kind of choice means that other people will be hurt, delayed, discouraged. The second group isn't as highly visible as the person in the doorway, but they are there, and management work is ministry to them. (By the way, I compromised with my tension. I told Mike I was very busy, but I would take a few minutes to talk with him right then. He graciously got right to the point, and I believe our brief conversation helped with his problem. Later I did follow up to see if we needed to talk further.)

Management is a supplement to leadership. Management is part of the work God calls the effective leaders to do in the church. There are many activities that God blesses as a supplement, that he condemns as a substitute. For example, the church which allows its music ministry to become the focal point of the church is in trouble with God. But surely God smiles on a music ministry that is a supplement to the central purposes of his church. Management should get the same treatment.

The church that suffers from management anemia will frustrate people. Interestingly, very few people will ever openly complain about the sickness; they just quit attending that church. Or worse, they keep attending and become content with mediocrity. The poorly managed church is easily spotted. Their sign on the front lawn needs to be relettered. The pastor's name has been printed where the last pastor's name appeared, and it is obvious since the blocking-out job was poorly done (the last pastor had a longer name). The sign posts are itching because grass is climbing their legs. At the church entry you notice that the door needs repainting, and the threshold is bent. Gum is stuck to the louvers of the threshhold. A solemn-faced usher hands you a bulletin but does not offer to seat you. You find your own way, sit down, and begin to read the mimeographed bulletin. The black ink is smudged on your copy. Several misspelled words leap from the page at you.

As you glance around you see a communion cup left from a previous service. The pencil in the book rack has no lead showing. The hymnal is tattered. Finally the service begins (three minutes late) when several men walk onto the platform. At announcement time the audience is told about two corrections in the bulletin. The ladies' circle will meet on Wednesday instead of Thursday. And the softball game will be at Patrick Park rather than Wasson Park as noted in the bulletin. When you are told that visitors should register, you notice that your pew rack is without visitors' cards.

At the end of the service you find the fellow who distributes the bulletins and ask him if you can have a copy of the church's constitution or doctrinal statement. He stares at you with open mouth and points toward the preacher. On Tuesday night the pastor comes to your home to answer your questions about the church. When you ask about the church's philosophy of working with children, it begins to freeze in your living room (although it is July). Pious words pile up until they flow under the door in a stream. But your question is not answered.

All the problems used to describe this particular church are *management problems*! They may be overlaid with other problems, but all can be solved by more efficient organization. Surely a church operating like the one in the preceding paragraphs will not be an attraction for the cause of Christ. Perhaps the first item on the agenda for change at your church is to simply do better what you are already doing. Maybe that is the best change you can help create in your church. Get organized! Make the buildings attractive. Be on time. Be accurate. Be reliable. Operate the church so that when people are told that the class will begin at 9:30 A.M. in Room 101 it begins at 9:30 A.M. in Room 101 and everyone knows it will because that's the way your church operates.

Rensis and Jane Gibson Likert have an amusing chart in their book, *New Ways of Managing Conflict*. The organizational chart shows the leader as Moses. On the next level the boxes are marked "agriculture, banking, complaints" and so on. In every box is the name "Moses." On the third level there appear eight more boxes such as "farming, justice, livestock." In every box on this level is the name "Moses." Forty-nine boxes outline the various necessary tasks in Israel, and Moses' name is in every box. In a graphic way the chart makes its point. It's the point Jethro stuck to his son-in-law. Delegate!

Written job descriptions for every task in the church help create change in an orderly way. Now please don't take it upon yourself to sit down and write all the job descriptions. Those sheets of paper will remain forever that—sheets of paper. They could achieve the status of "manual" and never be examined until the next pastor discovers them and demotes them to the round file in the corner. A better approach is to ask each person serving in the church to help you write his own job description. Is it too obvious to say that no one knows that job better than the one doing it? Each one can write the job description according to a simple format: job title, general responsibilities, specific responsibilities, responsible to, responsible for, relationships. If some people don't know the answers to those questions, it is time to discover the answers. When you've collected all the job descriptions, edit them, put them in a consistent form, and begin to use them.

When approached properly, people usually are not threatened by being asked to write a job description. Instead they feel complimented. Of course if the leader allows anyone to feel as though he is being asked to justify his position, the church may lose some volunteers. But if the leader wisely communicates, "Your position in this church is so important that we need to know exactly what you are doing and how you fit into the larger picture, and we need your help in making those determinations," happy response will follow.

Written job descriptions help people realize that their job is important. Also, they are useful when you recruit new people. It is impressive to be handed a job description when asked to teach the third-grade girls' Sunday school class. The job description answers questions and clarifies responsibilities, authority, and relationships. Many problems never arise because the job description has made clear what would otherwise be foggy in people's minds. A lot of misunderstandings ("I thought it was my responsibility to choose my own lessons") and conflict ("Who is he to tell me I must complete this roll book each week?") are bushwacked at the pass and never get into the church when you use well-written job descriptions.

Every reasonable church leader realizes that he can't teach every class and do every chore in the church. But many have not realized that good delegation is the way to manage what must be done. Part of the process is telling people in plain words what they are to do, how they are to do it, and what resources are available to them to assist in this particular task. Create a job description for everyone—volunteer and staff—who serves in the church. Include the pastor too.

The following list from J. D. Batten has application to the leader who wants to use good management to help facilitate change in the church.

1. Let each worker know where he stands; do not fail to discuss his performance with him periodically.
2. Give credit where credit is due—commensurate with accomplishments.
3. Inform workers of changes in advance. Informed workers are more effective.
4. Let workers participate in plans and decisions affecting them.
5. Gain your workers' confidence; earn their loyalty and trust.
6. Know all your workers personally. Find out their interests, habits, and touchy points—and capitalize on your knowledge of them.
7. Listen to your subordinates' proposals—they have good ideas too.
8. If a man's behavior is unusual for him, find out why. There is always a reason.
9. Try to make your wishes known by suggestion or request whenever possible. People generally don't like to be pushed.
10. Explain the why of things that are to be done. Workers do a better job then.
11. When you make a mistake, admit it and apologize. Others will resent your blaming someone else.
12. Show workers the importance of every job, thus satisfying the need for security.
13. Criticize constructively; give reasons for your criticism and suggest ways in which performance can be improved.
14. Precede criticisms with mention of the person's good points; show him you are trying to help him.
15. Do as you would have your people do. The supervisor sets the style.
16. Be consistent in your actions; let your workers be in no doubt as to what is expected of them.
17. Take every opportunity to demonstrate pride in the group. This will bring out the best in them.
18. If one man gripes, find out his grievance. One man's gripe may be the gripe of many.
19. Settle every grievance if at all possible; otherwise the whole group will be affected.
20. Set short and long range goals by which people can measure their progress.
21. Back up your workers. Authority must accompany responsibility.[26]

Although Likert created a facetious organizational chart as a dramatic way to emphasize the need to delegate, we should not think that organizational charts are jokes. Such a chart can be a useful tool in your church. This kind of chart visually represents people and the tasks they perform in the structure. Relationships among the people who perform the tasks in the structure are understandable at a glance if you have a properly drawn chart. Church chart makers make several common errors, however. Often Christians include their theology in the chart. For example, they may show God or Christ at the top. That confuses the purpose of the chart. That is theology. It has no place on an organizational chart. (Do I need to be defensive and say that I, too, believe that Christ *is* the head of the church?) Furthermore, Scripture verses and other rationale have no valid position on tools such as an organizational chart. Church polity need not appear either.

A common problem occurs when someone decides to create such a chart, and begins by dragging out a copy of the church constitution. Church constitutions are usually written by people who know very little about people, relationships, or communication. If the authors of most church constitutions intended that their works never be read—they are successful! Trying to draw an organizational chart from a constitution is like trying to put together your kid's new bike while following the directions for replacing a gear in your car's automatic transmission. Sure, the constitution may supply some general relationships, but then one should draw the chart according to the general understanding of those involved in the structure.

The process may reveal that there is no general understanding—and that is a good matter for discussion. When those foggy issues are resolved, you are on your way to a healthier, happier organization. The point is that such discussion needs to surface when the issue is "How do we draw this chart?" It's far less traumatic then than if you wait to discuss the issue when the question is "Can Pete make that decision?" or "Is Alice really in charge?" or "Does Sandra have the authority to reverse the committee's decision?"

When an organizational chart is created you should distribute a copy to each person represented on the chart—and to no one else. The general church public does not need to see the chart. They'd wonder why there's no theology on the chart. And they'd need several pages of instruction to properly understand the chart, although a chart should be self-explanatory to the persons represented on it.

The best way to draw a chart is to show the hierarchy in your church—who is responsible to/for whom. Each box should contain a title and a person's name. Resist the temptation to place boards and committees in the boxes. (That's the most common error in churches.) The trustees or deacons are responsible for the grounds committee, which is responsible for the building committee, which is responsible for the chair committee. That is the reason God's work gets done so slowly and poorly. Make an individual responsible for each task. Make a person responsible for a person.

Now don't think I am going to write some sarcastic words about committees. Personally I don't appreciate all those lame jokes about committees. I believe that many of God's people do great service for the Lord by serving on committees. It is an affront to fine Christians to poke fun at the concept of committees. But we must make sure that we use committees in the right way. These groups are at their worst when trying to make a decision. They function best when they discuss and give opinions. A good organizational chart shows the good procedure of one individual responsible for another. Alongside the person box you may use a dotted line leading to a committee box. That demonstrates that the committee is to advise that individual in that role. But the individual in the box has a task to perform which is identified by his title.

So the minister of education, Jack Diddle, is responsible for vacation Bible school. Below his box is a line leading to Jan Jones, V.B.S. director. Alongside his box is a dotted line showing that his advisory committee is the Christian education committee. And alongside Miss Jones' box is a dotted line demonstrating that she is advised and helped by a V.B.S. committee. This structure is superior to the one that shows the C.E. committee being responsible for the V.B.S. committee.

THIS   **NOT THIS**

| C.E. Minister Jack Diddle | C.E. Committee | | C.E. Committee |
| V.B.S. Director Jan Jones | V.B.S. Committee | | V.B.S. Committee |

This approach to organization facilitates change for the whole church. It is always easier for individuals than for committees to recognize the need for change and take action. Too often one set-in-cement brother or sister on a committee can stymie a worthwhile project for months. But this approach lessens the number of people the change agent must persuade about the changes he sees as important. It allows the leader who wants change to get things done even if one or two oppose a proposal. If he can persuade the individuals in the line relationships on the organizational chart, those individuals will then be responsible to persuade their own respective committees of the value of the idea.

This approach is not to bypass or manipulate any form of church government or polity. It is a common sense way of organizing the church for effective action and change. Almost any church with any form of church government or theology can operate on this basis without the trouble of changing its constitution, bylaws, or other documents. It's a tool, an approach, that does not impinge upon the deeper matters of polity or the authority of the Scriptures.

John Stratton was a good chairman of his church's Christian education committee. Last December he got the idea that next summer his church should initiate a camping program for nine- to twelve-year-old children. He chatted with the pastor, who thought the idea had merit. The church had only one staff member, so the pastor suggested that John pursue his idea through the C.E. committee. At the January C.E. committee meeting John laid his vision on the table for his fellow committee members. They responded warmly. Several made immediate suggestions about where, how, who, and cost. But many questions remained unanswered. Could a church of their size really have an effective ministry of camping for juniors? Was any other church in the city doing a similar ministry? Would costs make the ministry prohibitive? Could the church subsidize the program? How many church children would participate? What about insurance? Transportation? Should the venture be evangelistic? What about personnel? Available parks? *Wow!* A lot of work had to be done in January and February if the program was to be launched by summer. John was a wise chairman. He knew that an individual, not a committee, had to be held responsible for gathering these facts. "Charles, you seem enthusiastic about this possibility and you have a boy in the fifth grade. Would you like to begin gathering some data?" "Sure," responded Charles. And on they went to the next item on the agenda. Do you recognize the major mistake Chairman John made?

Whenever you give responsibility, you must marry it to accountability. John should also have said, "Charles, how about giving me a report in two weeks on the availability of parks, the insurance costs, and what other churches are doing in the area? I'd like to have that by January 24. Is that agreeable?" Now Chuck is on the spot. He must agree publicly to meeting a deadline, negotiate another deadline, or back out of the responsibility. He is helped in knowing (1) exactly what is expected and (2) when it is expected. This process helps create change in an orderly fashion.

"Mike, I am ready for a bigger challenge. Is that wrong? What is involved in leading a larger church?" The questions came from the smiling face across the table from me. My friend was a young pastor who was successfully leading a small church. He had pastored the church for the five years since his seminary graduation. Now he felt he would like another challenge. As I offered a few suggestions about the trade-offs one makes when helping lead a larger ministry, his smile wore off. His eyes narrowed and wrinkles accented his brow, "I'm not sure I'm willing to make those trade-offs," he confessed. I smiled then. He probed, "What are you thinking?" "You will because you can," I pontificated.

Why do some people want change? Why does anyone want change, especially when the wheels are running on the tracks without squeaking, and the train is on time? Change always involves risks. Yet you are a person who wants to change things in your church. (I know that because only that kind of person would read this far.) The fact is that you, like my pastor friend, must lead in creating change to keep your own identity. You too will keep prodding yourself and others to change. You will because you must.

But the risks in change can be greatly minimized by proper planning. Too many changes too quickly make people feel insecure. None of us can operate unless we believe that certain matters won't change too rapidly, and that they won't change at all without our knowing it. That's reasonable. Remember that need when you start the ball down the hill for your change.

Crawford Greenwalt, a former president of DuPont, observed that the best agents of change are persons who first plan and then follow a relaxed schedule to facilitate that plan. Those who are frantic in their manner gather a following with greater difficulty. Every minute in planning saves three or four in execution. MacKenzie charts it like this:[27]

Planning Time	Time Required for Execution

Planning Time	Time Required for Execution

The fact is that in most controlled experiments the more time you spend in planning the less time you need for execution. And, more important, the better the performance in a total of less time.

It was a wise man who proclaimed the proverb: Good results without good planning come from good luck, not good management.

Very often churches hinder their own growth because they do not plan for larger facilities. There is a cause-effect relationship between facilities and numbers. For years I doubted the leaders of Christianity who declared that a church will not grow beyond 85 percent of the capacity of its facilities. That is, that when a church reaches an attendance that uses its facilities to 85 percent capacity, that church has reached its maximum potential for growth. After removing three walls, ridding the auditorium of children, and providing three morning services, I believe those statistics. Others who have enjoyed church growth also verify the validity of the 85 percent rule (some people use 80 percent). Planning is a big slice of the pie when one wants to experience the rich dessert of a growing church.

It is always amusing for me to watch those Christians who don't believe in planning, especially for anything so carnal (to them) as church growth or church buildings. Usually these people make their preference a spiritual matter. "We don't believe in church buildings." "The early church met in homes and so do we." "In fact, we don't even have a paid minister. We all share the load equally." What fun it is to watch God bless these dear folks and create growth. Soon their houses are too small to accommodate their group. So one dear lady will volunteer to take the children into a bedroom for a separate Bible class. (Never call it a "Sunday school class." That's what those "other, big churches" call their ministry to children.) Then the children's class is too large for one bedroom, so another saint takes some of the children (always the group is divided by age or sex just like the "others" do it) into another bedroom. As the group grows they decide it would be nice to meet in a local public school. Then someone suggests that all that rent money could be buying their own building. "Wouldn't that be a better use of God's money?" So a modest building with Sunday school rooms—excuse me, I mean Bible class rooms—is constructed.

But that may be the limit for such groups. From here on they usually do stick to their principles about bigness and buildings. They begin more house churches and construct additional modest buildings. All of that seems well and good until you realize that when they want to organize a Christian school for their children their buildings are not adequate to house such a venture. So where do they go? That's right. They go to the church which has planned for a Christian school, meets the city codes, and is doing a job for God.

Furthermore, since these groups have reached their toleration point on programing for children by allowing a Sunday school, they send their children to other churches for weekday club programs and vacation Bible school programs.

Now, I don't mean to be cynical toward fellow believers. If they don't wish to plan and do God's business in an organized way, that's their business. I really have no problems with Christians who choose that style. But where we change lanes is when they make their position more spiritual than the Christians who do plan and organize, and then they sponge off them! That is irresponsible.

The point is that God's work is done best when it is planned. Planning is simply determining a course of action for tomorrow. Be decisive and work on a plan to cause specific events to occur. How often do boards and committees meet in your church to solve the problems of *today* and maintain only what is *already* happening? When was the last time you sat in on a church meeting where people creatively planned for the *future*, making specific plans, setting dates, giving people assignments, and the group was excited about what was *going* to happen?

The one who wants to create change in the church must be an L.R.P.—a long-range planner. Before the new building is started, share your vision and plans for the next unit. Get the opinion leaders in your church excited about an idea and meet with them to plan the strategy to accomplish the task. Some leaders fail at this intersection because they are action-oriented people. They like to do rather than plan. But remember the above chart. Better planning produces more work in less time. Thinking must precede action if change is to be effective.

Evangelicalism is being littered today with the bodies of ministers of discipleship. Lots of churches want a discipleship emphasis. Many ministers want to help lead in this area. So these ministers and churches get together and hire a minister of discipleship. The problem is that sufficient planning has not taken place. Often the members of the church possess too wide a range of ideas about the term "discipleship." Some believe the newly added minister is to do the work of a minister of education. Others think he should help people memorize verses or teach home Bible studies. Some feel he is primarily a counselor. Some who help pay his salary believe he should work only with groups. Meanwhile, a group in the church wants him to be available only for one-to-one ministry. Some think he should occasionally preach while others feel he should only drink coffee and challenge Christians on a personal basis. *Slam! Bang! Ouch!* Ministers of discipleship and discipleship programs are being spit up like Jonah from the fish's stomach. Churches are being scorched on the term (maybe the idea) of discipleship. Ministers are being discouraged. And Christianity is hurting because of a lack of proper planning.

"Really, Myra, teaching the junior high class is not that hard. They are a good group of kids. And there aren't that many. Besides, here is the quarterly. Just read it and you'll do fine." And another teacher has been recruited. Myra will probably enter the class next Sunday with sweaty palms. Most likely she'll do poorly, know it, and quit soon. Like many Christians, she will resolve her guilt feelings and feelings of failure by sighing, "Teaching is just not my gift."

But the failure is not Myra's. The sign "Failure" should probably be hung around the neck of the one who recruited her without offering to train her. But it's likely that hanging such a sign around his neck would be too cruel since *he* was recruited for *his* job by the same method. The real issue is not to fix blame, but to provide a training program in your church.

One of the reasons people don't want to change is that they are not properly trained to do their tasks. They perform as they always have because that is the only way they know. Training doesn't have to begin big. It can begin small. You can start infor-mally with one person. Offer to train someone you think might be open to the idea. Go ahead. Try it. Already you expect that person to jump at the opportunity, don't you? But now you are beginning to think about the time it involves to train even one person. And you are right. It will take time. But is it worth it? Will training one person help you accomplish the desired changes in your church? When you train even one person, you will be closer to your goals for your church.

Perhaps you don't feel competent to train other Christians in a particular area. Well, you can feed that person some books and tapes that will help. Remember to make him accountable to read or listen and report back to you. You can take another person (how about a car-full?) to a nearby seminar or Sunday school convention.

A few years ago I decided that I would never learn to snow ski. Even though I live in "Ski Country U.S.A.," I concluded that one can't do everything in life, and skiing would just require more risk and money than I wanted to invest. Besides, I was involved in several other sports and recreational activities. My wife agreed with my logic. We both politely refused offers to go skiing. Then a family made us an offer we couldn't refuse. "Come share our condominium at no cost to you." Well, it was a $400-a-week palace at Snowmass (Aspen, Colorado). "Will you teach us how to ski?" I asked. "No," replied my friend, "but I'll get you and Nancy into the ski school." So we accepted their offer and enjoyed the fine accommodations. We were skillfully trained in snowplowing, turning, and boarding and dismounting the lifts. And, you guessed it, now we love skiing. The simple truth is that we got hooked because someone took an interest in us and was willing to help us get training.

You can find Christians in your church hiding behind the pews who refuse to be involved because the risk is too high. Minimize that risk by offering (Do we dare suggest requiring?) training before one begins a ministry. You can create a training program for committee members and workers at all levels which will help you create change in an orderly way in your church.

Five
PURPOSELY COMPROMISE FOR CHANGE

Ivor Richard, Great Britain's chief delegate to the United Nations, made this comment about the United States Bicentennial: "You are celebrating—and we are tolerating—certain events which occurred two hundred years ago and which, I hasten to add, we now recognize as probably irreversible." Great Britain is now willing to compromise its ideals and recognize that the United States is probably never going to be a British colony again.

One recent week brought another example of compromise. Several Christians came into my office to ask for help. Each was an alcoholic. Alcoholics? In this church? Yes, it was true. So I set about to help them. We started group meetings in my home. Zack, a member of the church with a great deal of experience in helping alcoholics, agreed to help me. The few of us met. Help was given. The members got off the sauce. More joined the group. A few women came. A new ministry was born.

This ministry was created because of compromise. It is my belief that the Bible calls drunkenness "sin." Yet I don't believe one can make an honest case from the Scriptures for total abstention. Certainly anyone who is an alcoholic should be a total abstainer. It would be easier to say to my alcoholic friends, "Look, pal, you claim to be a Christian, so act like one and get off the booze." But that isn't the way to handle the problem. That is the way most churches have handled the problem; therefore, people with drinking problems don't confide in the church for help. In fact, the more I've gotten involved in this matter, the more embarrassed I am at how poorly the church has done in helping with *the* major drug-abuse problem in this country. Only when we compromised our hard line and let people know that we cared, did we learn how many fine Christians who attend church and Bible studies have a drinking problem.

One of the first compromises Zack and I make when a new person joins our group is to get the individual on Anti-buse. This drug helps the drinker assure himself that he will not drink. If one does drink *any* alcohol within seventy-two hours of taking Anti-buse, he becomes violently ill. (Some of our group members have had the experience, and they've related in detail what happens.) Sure, it would be nicer to tell the people that they can quit drinking and pray and never drink again. But some have tried that many times, and it didn't work for them. The *reason* it didn't work is not important. The *fact* is, it didn't work! So we compromise and start our friends on Anti-buse rather than take the purist approach.

Many Christians fear any compromise. But the one who wishes to create change in the church must learn that compromise is not a dirty word. (Some of the material for this chapter was originally published by Tyndale in *The Church That Dared to Change*, chapter nine: "Compromise Is Not a Dirty Word.")

We are emerging from an era in which compromise ruined Christians, churches, and whole denominations. A few decades ago many of the mainline denominations began to compromise basic doctrines of Scripture. Many who were supposed to be prophets of God traded the Bible for psychology textbooks. On the other hand, many true Christians fought this kind of compromise and stayed within churches and denominations until they felt they had no impact, or were asked to leave. During those days many new denominations were created. Compromise brought dishonor to God, his Word and his church. Compromise kept people from truth and from heaven. In light of that, many Christians survived those denominational wars believing that compromise is a dirty word. Yet all of us compromise in many areas of life. The dictionary defines compromise as a "settlement in which each side gives up some demands or makes concessions."

Christians should be willing to compromise certain things with one another. No one gets his first choice all the time, so we must learn to follow the rules of compromise. Sure, there will be disagreements about color of new carpet, removal of a wall, singing of certain songs, use of buildings, choice of words, order of services, and multitudes of other matters. But still, Christians should not fight, argue, pout, or disrupt God's work. Emotionally mature people and groups make decisions in an orderly way. Willingness to compromise is part of Christian maturity. Compromise must be done with a smile, realizing that partial accomplishment is better than none.

Compromise simply means being willing to settle for less than the best in order to get the job done. Decisions must be made if progress is to be attained. Decisions should be based on available data. In the area of politics, as you look at any slate of candidates you discover that none is perfect. Maybe none of the candidates exerts a positive Christian influence. Therefore, you do the best you can by voting for the ones who seem to be closest to your particular political philosophy. That's better than not voting at all. You compromise by accepting less than the best.

On your job, you generally don't quit just because you have some problems. When you submit a requisition for so much of an item, but are offered less, you don't usually refuse to take *any*. You compromise and take what you get. When you ask for a raise of so much and are offered less, do you take it? Every sermon I preach is a compromise between available study time and my "purist" standards. I rarely meet my own standards for sermon preparation. I compromise and do the best I can in the time available.

If you have been married for any length of time you've discovered at least a few faults in your partner. Yet you don't throw away your marriage vows. You continue living and working with that person.

You compromise in your choice of churches. The church you belong to may be larger or smaller than you wish. It may not have an adequate young people's program or nursery facility. No matter what church you join, you compromise about something. That is preferable to not serving Christ through any church at all. Some wise man said, "If you ever find a perfect church, don't join it. You'll ruin it."

When you purchase a home or a car the salesman quotes a price. You offer less than that. You both realize that you will compromise before a price agreement can be reached. We compromise in many areas of life.

Compromisers populate the Bible. Paul was a compromiser. Paul never spoke against slavery. He wrote principles that demonstrated that it is wrong, yet he sent Onesimus to Philemon to continue as a slave. Paul told slaves to be good slaves. That was a compromise on his part. When Paul appealed to Caesar he was willing to stay in jail longer with a future chance of release. Paul accepted the sentence so he could make an appeal. A noncompromiser would have said, "I am innocent. Turn me loose." Paul compromised when he circumcised Timothy (Acts 16:1-3). In Acts 15 the Jerusalem Council declared that non-Jewish believers did not have to be circumcised. The next chapter records Paul circumcising Timothy. That was a compromise. In Acts 21:17-26 Paul returned to Jerusalem and took a Jewish vow at the request of James and the church leaders. Again Paul obviously compromised his position.

Not only did Jewish customs cause Paul to compromise but so did heathen customs. In 1 Corinthians 8 he made it clear that there was nothing wrong with eating idol meat. Yet he told the Christians in Corinth not to do it if it offended a brother. That was a compromise of his position.

Elisha was a compromiser. In 2 Kings 5, Naaman, the Syrian general, was healed of leprosy because he obeyed the Word of the Lord through Elisha. In verses 15-17, Naaman offered a gift to Elisha which Elisha refused. Then the Syrian general declared that he was taking some dirt back to his home so that he, too, could worship Jehovah. In verse 19 Elisha said, "Go in peace." Elisha compromised his position. He didn't try to straighten Naaman out by telling him that soil from Israel wasn't necessary to worship God. A mature Christian can allow an immature Christian the privilege of mistakes in the process of growth.

God compromised with Israel and gave them a king against his perfect will (1 Samuel 8). God also compromised with Moses and did not blot out the nation for their sin. He only punished them.

Jesus compromised in the incarnation. He was willing to become man, talk with humans, and even die at the hands of evil men. Jesus paid taxes (Matthew 17:24-27). Does God owe man taxes? Certainly not. Jesus compromised his position. Jesus didn't speak against slavery. On one occasion he told his disciples, "I have many things to tell you but you can't bear them now." I interpret that to mean, "I will compromise and not tell you all the truth you really need."

In some areas we can't compromise. It is wrong to compromise clearly taught doctrines and absolutes of the Bible. We cannot compromise on the doctrines of the virgin birth, the inspiration of the Scriptures, and the necessity for individual salvation. We cannot compromise the fact that the Bible is the absolute authority with some absolute rules. It is never right to lie, cheat, steal, or commit adultery. We should never compromise clear doctrines or absolutes.

Nor should convictions based on clear revelation and clear principles be compromised. Even subjective convictions based on our background, teaching, or training should not be compromised if the compromise would harm us or make us feel guilty. This principle is found in 1 Corinthians 8. Paul said that although it is not wrong in general to eat idol meat, it would be wrong in certain cases. A weaker Christian might think he could eat idol meat, and then, having done it, might feel guilty. Paul said that this would make the brother stumble. The principle is that we are not to transgress our own convictions (even those not based on clearly taught principles of the Word) if it causes us to feel guilty. We should remember, however, that it is not wrong for these kinds of convictions to change with more light.

In other areas we can compromise. We can compromise a lesser conviction for a greater one, but not a lesser absolute for a greater absolute. In other words I am not saying that it is ever okay to lie in order to love. If you have a conviction about a matter in your church and the church does otherwise, you should compromise your lesser conviction for the greater conviction you have about church unity. An elderly woman in our church came to me declaring that she was upset about our opening a coffee house to reach "far-out" young people. She said that she didn't believe in it and was opposed to it. But she concluded her remarks by saying, "Pastor, here is five dollars for that ministry." That's compromise of the right kind.

We should compromise by being willing to work with those who don't hold our convictions, in order to continue working with them and influencing them. Paul worked with the Jews in the synagogue who did not hold his convictions. In one of our southern states I was once the pastor of a church which held a segregationist viewpoint. I compromised my position by not allowing black people to join that church, but I wouldn't compromise my position by keeping black people from worshiping in that church. I was willing to make the compromise so that I could continue working and influencing those believers for Jesus Christ. We are not called of God to straighten everyone out.

We should also compromise in the standards we want other people to live up to. In spite of the qualifications for deacons given in 1 Timothy 3, we do take less. The church I lead had an ideal of a perfect pastor, but they took less when they accepted me. Unless it is a clear violation of a scriptural absolute or principle, take what God gives you: compromise.

Several principles should guide us in the matter of compromise. First, remember that you might be wrong. In 2 Samuel 16, David was fleeing Jerusalem because his son Absalom was taking over the city with an army. On his way out of the city, Shimei cursed David and threw rocks at him. One of David's soldiers, Abishai, said, "David, let me remove his head." David said "no" in verse 10, declaring that God had told Shimei to do what he was doing. In chapter 19 David returned to Jerusalem after defeating Absalom, and Shimei went to him at the river and apologized. Again Abishai wanted to remove his head, and again David denied him that privilege. David concluded by saying, "Now I know I am to be the king of Israel." David had some good indications that he was God's anointed king, yet he was not sure that he was always right or even that God was continuing to have his hand upon him. One reason people fail to see the scriptural principles about compromise is that they are always so sure they are right.

Once a metropolitan pastor was hot to change the structure of his church. Frankly, he had some good ideas. But he wouldn't compromise. He wanted his changes "right now." When the church wasn't ready to move that quickly, he became disgruntled. He dug in and pulled out the common weapon Christians so often use on one another: "I'm more spiritual than you because I can see we need to make this change now, and you don't agree with me." Unfortunately, this individual had deceived himself into thinking that the lay leaders of the church were solidly behind him. He made his move and was utterly crushed to learn that he had almost no support. The ugly result was that he left the ministry of the church and became bitter for a time about the whole affair. In retrospect, it is easy to see that this brother made the mistake of not being willing to compromise. He certainly could have continued to make many wonderful contributions to the body if he just had not been so pushy in that one area.

His leaving the church forced the church board into a compromise. They were quite disturbed at his actions. But they decided to graciously give him seven weeks' severance pay, even though he had been employed by the church less than a year. When he didn't find another position within that time, he brazenly asked the board for another seven weeks' pay. The board members were livid. They could compromise no further. They quickly and unanimously voted to deny his request.

Another principle to remember is that we all compromise in different areas. Don't be quick to condemn others. We can't crawl into the head of another person and know why he's doing what he's doing. It's difficult for anyone else to know his convictions and background. Our tendency is to wrap our self-righteous robes around us when we see someone compromise in an area where we do not. We should resist that temptation.

This is one of the biggest problems I face in marriage counseling. One person believes that inconsistency is the biggest sin in town. Meanwhile, his partner believes that lack of affection is the crux of all evil. And of course, one is very consistent and unaffectionate while the other is very affectionate and inconsistent. So neither wants to compromise his own ideals or let the other manifest his faults.

"We believe the ministry is people, so let's hire more church staff to minister to people." "No, no, no. We must erect a new building in order to minister to more people. We can't afford more staff this year." Someone had better compromise or conflict will result on that one. The truth is that individuals and families spend their money very differently from each other. But when it comes to spending money in the church, all the members feel that their priorities should be observed. If the church is in financial problems and needs to reduce its expenditures, the people with little children will vote to reduce the ministry to teen-agers but not to reduce the paid help in the nursery. Some will push to go ahead and purchase the air-conditioning unit, but delay the purchase of the new organ. The wise leader will recognize these situations, confront them, explain them, and lead the church into unity through compromise.

And, by all means, the leader must insist that one group not get super-pious and pull the old "my-idea-is-more-spiritual-than-your-idea" routine. My guess is that normal conflict which can be handled in business, government, and labor situations through compromise can become war in a church where people use a super-saint approach. When one declares that God is on his side in the conflict, the opponent must then do the same. Opinions become convictions. The faith is suddenly on the line. Compromise (as well as unity and progress) is no longer an option. Worthwhile change has lost the battle.

A third principle is to balance the teaching of the compromise with the teaching of separation in your own life. Don't use the teaching of compromise as an excuse for sin.

Compromise is not sin. It is God's method of progress. Many churches miss God's best because they aren't willing to allow progress in due course. The Christian and the church that must have purity "right now" in all areas of life usually end up discomfited. The ones not willing to compromise and face reality become frustrated. And frustrated Christians breed frustrated Christians, not spiritual Christians. If you want to create change in your church, be willing to accept modest beginnings. Don't hold out for the whole package all at once. Realize that any change must have a beginning, and accept small encouragements. Thank God for any little willingness to change that any of the pillars show.

My first Sunday at my present church I decided that the beautiful wooden border on the top of the pulpit would have to go. Only my eyebrows peeked above that monster. I really wanted a whole new pulpit. But that decorative pulpit had been there much longer than I had. It fit into the motif and design of all the chancel furniture. But it was evidently designed by an architect who didn't want to see preachers, not by a preacher who wants to communicate with gestures and words. I compromised. I asked only that the border on top be removed. The board agreed. Then, several years later, I mentioned to a friend that I had always wanted a transparent pulpit. I want people to understand that "here we are together, people and pastor, to learn God's Word." My friend told me that three houses away from the church was a man whose business was making Plexiglas objects. I left the conversation and walked to the man's house. He invited me into his home and identified himself as a Christian. Before I left he had taken me to his basement workshop and built a model for a custom-made Plexiglas pulpit. The first compromise was worth the wait. For years I have enjoyed that beautiful, clear pulpit. In fact, our weekly printed sermons are titled, "The Plexiglas Pulpit." The craftsman who made the structure is now in the church with his family. The follow-up story is that recently I've learned to preach without any piece of furniture between the congregation and myself.

The point is that to have removed that first wooden structure and replaced it with the Plexiglas pulpit several years ago would have been too much change too quickly. But the slow progress from wood to Plexiglas to fresh Colorado air was accepted step by step.

It is not right to do wrong in order to get a chance to do right. But it is right to do half-right in order to get a chance to do more right. And it is right to do things that are neither right nor wrong in order to get a chance to do right. Compromise is not a dirty word.

Six
PROMOTE
BIG GOALS

Southdale was once a thriving evangelical church on the edge of a metropolitan area. The people were excited when the church was first started as a branch from a downtown ministry. At first the church grew very rapidly. The neighborhood was expanding and the group assembled in the local public school. Then they were able to purchase property in an ideal location. The mother church helped with the purchase, and the ground soon belonged to Southdale. The church grew on. In a few years the group was able to sell church bonds, negotiate a small loan, and build a small facility on their property. This move stimulated the growth of the church even further. They were reaching others for Christ, and the people were happy with God's blessing upon their church.

Southdale then set a major goal of building a large auditorium. For several years they saved, planned, and prayed about the new auditorium. Soon the new building was the topic of all conversation. Rarely was there a Sunday morning service without some emphasis upon the eventual sanctuary. Then the big day came when the church broke ground and watched the new auditorium grow. The auditorium grew and the people were ecstatic that their long-range goal was about to be reached. In only eleven months the building was complete. They had a grand celebration. On the first Sunday morning in the new structure the pastor was nervous, the choir was nervous, and the people were jittery. Soon, however, no one was nervous. In fact, in only a few months no one was even excited. Southdale Church began to decline. The zest had left the congregation. They had met their goal, and there was no place to go.

Southdale today still sits on the edge of the metropolis. Now houses surround it. But the auditorium is less than half full each Sunday morning. Several pastors have come and gone since that beautiful building was built. Those who know the church best are unified in their evaluation of the problem: Southdale had a building as its goal—and when its goal had been met, the church began to die.

How sad it often is to see pastors leave a ministry after a church building goes up. For years this phenomenon was blamed upon the squabbling that often takes place during a building program, but closer scrutiny has revealed that the problem more often is the emotional and spiritual letdown that occurs when a goal is reached. That emotion strikes especially when the goal was not one that merited as much time, energy, and creativity as were put into it.

The one who wishes to create change in an orderly fashion from within the church must realize that he has never arrived at a final stage. He will not allow the church to feel that it has "arrived" either. He knows that the really important tasks are never finished. Spiritual goals are ongoing. Certainly there are some goals that can be reached in this life, and most assuredly we should set goals that can be reached. Yet the one who thinks that after he has reached those he will be happy, has lost sight of the ultimate goals for life and ministry.

The truth is that a group of people must know what they want and how they are going to get it. Organization is simply people working together to accomplish something, but those people must know what they are working *for* in order to be truly effective. They do not have to have a goal in order to work together, but they will soon disperse and certainly be unhappy unless they realize what the goals are in front of them.

A church that wants to inspire people to rise to the heights that God has called believers to, must set goals that are beyond new buildings, organs, pianos, and sculptured lawns. Certainly God is not against any of those things, but those are simply by-products of the real goals and attitudes that must hold the attention of God's people. The possibility thinker, Robert Schuller, puts it nicely:

Set successful goals and you will succeed. Fail to set successful goals and you can be assured of failure. Success or failure starts at this point, for goal setting is nothing more than planning ahead. And when you fail to plan, you plan to fail.[28]

"No one wants to help around this church. Only a few of the members are carrying the load for the entire group." These and other such statements are often heard by those who are faithfully serving in the local church. But if some people are not serving the church, then those who are serving have a responsibility to discover the real core of the problem. Perhaps it is that people are uncommitted to Jesus Christ. Perhaps it is that people are not well trained. Maybe part of the problem is a lack of challenge. Maybe some in the congregation need teaching concerning the nature of the church and the truth of spiritual gifts. But perhaps there is another reason that the leaders do not want to face. It is a tough problem. Confronting this possibility is threatening to even the most secure church leader. But maybe . . . just maybe it is true: *Our goals are so shallow and trite that we bore people.*

Could it be that there are capable people in the congregation who simply ignore the church (other than Sunday morning attendance) because the goals we set for the local assembly are neither big nor important? In some cases, maybe those who attend and do not get involved do not even have the vaguest notion what the goals of their church really are.

"Leaders must lead," explained Dr. Russell Shive, a denominational leader. That simple statement was explained to me during the tenure of my first pastorate. Somehow or other, it gripped my life and has made a profound difference in the way I do things. Years after Dr. Shive made that statement and explained it to me, I was asked to deliver a seminar on the art of effective leadership. I built it around that very simple statement—leaders must lead. The truth is that leaders must be visionaries. If leaders are not leading, no one will lead. If leaders are not visionaries, no one will see beyond the horizon. Unless people occasionally shake their heads at you and call you "crazy," then you are not doing your job! Jesus Christ set the largest possible goal before his disciples when he challenged them to go into *all the world*. What bigger goal could Jesus have given his followers?

Certain simple steps are essential in goal setting for your church. The first step is to *chart your history*. Each year I deliver a "state of the church address." In this Sunday morning message I first explain to the congregation where we have been in the last twelve months. The response to this approach has been most encouraging. Even those who have dropped into the church for the first time find it helpful to know about the emphasis and ministries of this local congregation. Those who have been an integral part of the church become warmly enthused to see what God has done in the past 365 days. And those who are new to the church use the annual address as an opportunity to catch up.

Learning about the history of one's own denomination and tradition is very important. Probably these matters should not be dwelt upon at length, but none the less it is good to know one's ecclesiastical roots. Even those churches which claim to be strictly independent can trace the history of evangelicalism and identify with the people, movements, and missions of their past.

Attendance is not the only historical measuring device, but it may be one valid way to judge one's growth. Surely, if one is involved in gimmicks and games in order to hustle bodies into the church building and Sunday school rooms, then attendance records are not so important. But if one does not take that approach to the ministry and, rather, sees the ministry as an attempt to help people spiritually without tricking them into attending church, then attendance may be a guide. It is helpful to see where one has been in the last year with the matter of attendance. Checking attendance month by month against former years will help the congregation to see what has been taking place.

Giving may also be a valid measurement. Show the congregation what they have given in the last twelve months as compared with previous years. You may also wish to check matters such as specialized giving to missions or particular groups. Each church will have to determine what it thinks is important to use as a standard of measurement. Some churches keep records concerning conversions or baptisms or new memberships. All of these may be shown to the congregation as it charts its history in order to set its goals for the future. It may be important to some churches to chart the ages of those who are members of the church, or perhaps to simply look at those who have joined the church in the past twelve months and take special note of their age groups.

Any healthy body needs a balanced diet. A wise and sensitive dietician will provide that balanced diet for those he loves. The pastor who wants to feed his people spiritually will provide a spiritual diet that is well balanced between the Old and New Testaments, doctrine, narrative, historical, and poetic writings. This should also be shown to the congregation as they look over what they have accomplished in the past twelve months. It may surprise the congregation (and perhaps the pastor) to see an overview of what has been delivered from the pulpit on fifty-two Sundays. This again is a first step in charting one's course for the future.

If the church has experienced unusual growth or decline, it is good to note that in an honest and forthright manner and make observations concerning the possible reasons for the unusual growth pattern.

Defining one's ministry is the second step in setting goals. Every group of church leaders should work together to create a definition of the church. It is amazing how many people who have been involved in the church for years have never taken time to define the church. You should define the church according to your own theology and understanding of the Scriptures. For our purposes we use this definition: "The church is the body of Christ consisting of every born-again believer and is expressed when a group of believers assemble regularly, designate leaders, observe the ordinances, and promote worship, evangelism, discipleship, and fellowship." Furthermore, it is important that each church carefully define its own distinctives. You do believe that you are different from the church that meets a block away. You are in a particular denomination (or not in any denomination) because you believe in your distinctives. There are matters that you hold to be important. You should define those for the congregation so that they know why they are Presbyterian, Lutheran, Episcopalian, or independent.

Even more detail is necessary in this step of definition. Not only are you a member of a certain denomination which makes you different from the church down the street, but your particular church is different from all the rest of the churches in your

denomination or who are part of the tradition that you hold.
Therefore, the church leaders need to carefully define what is
different about your particular church as compared with other
churches that are very much like yours in theology and approach.
This will again help in setting goals.

Every church has a personality. All have strengths and weak-
nesses. That's why people come to your church. You meet needs
that others do not. Even further definition must be approached
by listing all of the ministries of your church. You may be surprised at how many ministries you really do have. Perhaps most of
the believers in your assembly think that all you offer is a Sunday
morning, Sunday night, and midweek service in addition to Sunday school. But when you think through all that is going on, you
will probably be pleasantly surprised at how many ministries are
being developed through your fellowship. Defining these and
categorizing them (however you wish to categorize them) will
assist you in the next step.

More and more churches are no longer content to allow people
to join their memberships just to have their names on the roll. If
membership is important in your church, then you need to define
what membership involves. If it does simply involve getting a
name on a roll or "transferring a letter" (where did that tradition
ever begin?), then you need to admit that. Growing churches are
now realizing that membership involves a commitment. In our
own situation, we have attempted to make each new member
realize that membership involves responsibilities. Those
responsibilities are three:

1. To allow others to know and love you.
2. To love and care for others.
3. To be trained for ministry.

A third step toward setting goals that will help you create
orderly change from within the church is to *evaluate your context*.
We know, for instance, that the current population of El Paso
County (Colorado) is 240,000. For 1980 the projected figure is
376,000; and by 1990 the county planners are expecting 511,000

people to live in our county. It is important for us to know what to expect in terms of the future in our own place. The median age of our county has moved from 25.8 to 24.2 in the last sixteen years. That does not seem like a significant change, yet it does indicate a trend. This too helps us evaluate what is happening in our community and learn how to communicate with the people around us. The present median age of 24.2 in our county is compared with a median age of 27.0 in our state and 28.8 in the nation as a whole. Again, these figures help us realize what is happening in our own community as compared with the larger state and nation.

Other figures also help us understand how we should approach the work of the ministry in years to come. Recent figures reveal that by the year 2000 all age groups will be significantly increased, but the age group from birth to nineteen years of age will increase only 8 percent while the group from age sixty-five up will increase 30 percent. Meanwhile, the largest percentage of growth will be with those in the age group of thirty-five to forty-nine. That age group will increase 65 percent. Immediately one sees that future emphasis will not be on children and teen-age ministries, but on middle-age and senior citizen ministries, if the church is going to properly reach its society for Christ. This is a dramatic change in our approach. You know of many churches that have young people's ministers, but how many have a minister to middle adults or senior citizens?

As the future is carefully analyzed by sociologists, Christians must learn to "discern the times" and adjust their ministries appropriately. Most futurologists agree that in our country there will be more and more apartment living. What will that do for the ministry of your church? What is your church doing now to reach people living in the apartments that have already been built in its neighborhood? As our country faces more shortages, smaller families are predicted. This will affect the church. Projections indicate that there will be more working women. This will affect a great portion of each congregation. If women will be working more, what will that do to your women's Bible studies and mission societies? And what will it do to the children's ministries of your church?

Another prediction is that more people will be married later in life. If that is so, how will you make good use of the young adults in the ministry of your church before they do get married? Already we are seeing one prediction come true: that the divorce rate will increase. What is your church's position on the matter of divorce, and how will you minister to this large segment of society in the future? If it is true, as is being predicted, that there will be more childless couples, will your church be ready to meet the challenge of these people? Is it acceptable that our churches are becoming more family oriented and less oriented toward single parents and childless couples?

The social prophets tell us that Americans will be less mobile in the coming years. Already the slowdown in moving has begun. How will that affect *your* community and *your* ministry? There is going to be more public education, as well as more college education. People are going to go to school more on a part-time basis, but for a continued number of years through their lifetimes. Will that affect your services at church, and are you prepared to meet the challenge of the change of schedule being faced by your congregation? The American work week is predicted to be down to thirty-four hours by 1985. People already are doing less hard manual labor, and they have more discretionary time. As that becomes increasingly true, how will the church meet the challenge?

Fewer large cars will use the highways in the future. What will that mean for your youth retreats and other transportation events of the church? If it is true that there is going to be less TV watching and more out-of-doors activities, how will you arrange your ministry to meet that challenge? If people do continue to fear crime and travel, will you be willing to adjust your Sunday evening service appropriately? If inflation continues to take a larger chunk from the paychecks of your members, how will you be willing to adjust your church budget? And if utility costs continue to increase and money becomes as tight as predicted, would you be willing to have multiple services in your church building rather than build a new structure?

All of these questions are pertinent to your goal setting. You cannot properly set goals until you have charted your history, defined your ministry, and evaluated your own setting.

Surveys can be very helpful to understanding what your particular church believes is important. Unfortunately many church leaders operate for years on the assumption that they know the people and the makeup of their own congregations, when in fact they do not. In Appendix A (pages 181 through 185), you will find a sample survey that was successfully used in one church. The form on pages 181, 182 was first mailed to every member. The cover letter explained that the member was to look over an enclosed sheet that listed all the ministries of his church. He was asked then to check in the appropriate places to show whether he felt each ministry was a strength, needed to be changed, or needed a new emphasis. Perhaps none of those three apply to certain ministries. Then no observation should be made. The cover letter told the member that soon an interviewer would call him, make an appointment, and come to his home to talk about the observations he made on the form. The interviewer would than ask additional questions and make comments as the member explained his observations. These were recorded on the form on page 183. Next, all of the comments made about any particular ministry were combined and given to the person in charge of that ministry. That person then was obligated to complete another form (shown on pages 184 and 185) and return it to the church leaders. In addition, that leader received a list of names of all who were interested in working in his particular area of ministry.

This approach allowed the church leaders to know what every member thought was important about every part of the ministry of the church. It also gave every member a personal opportunity to express himself to an individual and not just on a sheet of paper. Furthermore, everyone in charge of any ministry in the church received a tremendous amount of feedback about his ministry. This helped him to understand what he was doing right or wrong. It also revealed that many ministries had not been adequately explained to the congregation. A tremendous amount of misinformation was floating about.

For several years we thought we knew the composite makeup of a typical "average" member of our church. However, when we took a simple survey one Sunday morning, we were surprised in several areas. Visual observation does not tell the church leaders all that they need to know. The result of a recent survey in our own context is provided in the Appendix (page 186). It was this survey that revealed that 83 percent of our congregation regularly attended a weekday Bible study. We concluded, therefore, that we need no longer feel guilty about our own church mid-week Bible study having such a poor attendance. In fact we discontinued that Bible study.

It is probably wise every few years to make a rather extensive survey that provides the congregation an opportunity to express itself and its needs. The tools for such surveys can be found through Sunday school curriculum publishing houses and denominational headquarters. It is always fun to put the results of these surveys on computer cards and run crisscrosses of the results. This allows one to see how those who are above a certain age answered the question and how those below a certain age answered the same question. It also allows one to see the difference between how new believers and more mature believers have answered a particular question.

Before a Christian can effectively help his church establish its goals he must work at establishing his own personal goals. At least once a year every Christian leader needs to evaluate what he is trying to accomplish in several areas of his life. A simple one-page chart will help you determine where you are going and how you intend to get there. For beginners it is well to deal simply in five basic areas: spiritual (personal), ministry, physical, family, and the church I help lead. Write out your goals for one year, three years, and eight years in each of those five areas. The entire process can be done on one 8½" x 11" page.

Think hard; be specific; don't bluff. If you cannot think of a specific, clear goal in the area of your physical life for eight years from now, then simply leave that space blank. Ask the question, "What *specifically* do I want to accomplish in this area of my life in this time frame?" Like most people, you will probably be surprised when you take this simple approach. You will learn that simply writing your goals will help you aim toward those goals. Probably they will not be part of the conscious framework upon which you hang your hat every day; yet they will become part of the unconscious network of your entire fabric.

In addition, every serious Christian leader should establish his own priorities in the work of the ministry. I have found through the years that it helps to put my overall goal of ministry before me. Where I do the majority of my work and study I have a little sign that tells me what my job is. On that same sign I have listed five priorities for the work of the ministry. Several times a day I look at that sign and ask, "Mike, is what you are doing right now directly related to your job, and how high on the priority scale is this task?" That approach helps keep me on target.

The effective church will take the time to hammer out its own goals. The end result should be a simple, terse statement that helps the leadership and the entire congregation to understand what it is trying to do. Most successful churches in America have done the hard work that this step requires. One church simply says that its goal is evangelism and discipleship. Another church states it as being "to bring people to maturity in Christ." This particular church then explains that it uses three methods to develop that goal: evangelism (salvation), discipleship (personal walk), and training (ministry). However you state it in your church, it must be stated.

A list of continuing goals has helped the work of the ministry in the church where God has allowed me to labor. These goals are not as specific as annual goals, yet they do help the entire church remember what it is trying to do in seven specific areas: spiritual growth, evangelism, education, fellowship, community, music, and missions (See 187 and 188).

Annual goals are an absolute necessity for the church that wants to reach its community and world for Christ. These goals need to be formed by the leaders of the church. A leadership retreat or staff retreat or a series of scheduled sessions is essential to forming a list of productive annual goals. Again, the goals should be specific, visionary, and led by the Spirit. As the church leaders determine the mind of God and work out their common goals, they must remember not to be shackled by human reasoning. Do not fail to establish a goal simply because you lack finances, facilities, or personnel. Believe God! Think big! Dream! Determine what you believe God wants you to do through the ministry of your church. Then establish that goal in a written form. Seek God to determine if it truly is God's heart to accomplish that goal within the next twelve months through your church. As that goal is confirmed, share it with others. Then challenge the entire church with the concept. Always ask the right questions when setting goals:

1. What are we doing?
2. What do we want to accomplish?
3. How can we do it?

Writing the goal is, of course, only the beginning. It is an important step, but many more steps must be taken to see that goal accomplished. The leaders who establish the annual goal need to plot specifically how that goal is to be accomplished. It helps to put a time frame on these steps. Perhaps a goal will need to be accomplished through certain exposures of the congregation. Those exposures may come through preaching, through group meetings, and/or through articles in the bulletin or church newsletter. It is extremely discouraging to any group at a retreat or meeting to establish significant goals and then never see anyone follow up on the goals to work toward their accomplishment. It helps to assign specific people to carry out specific steps toward the pursuit of each goal. These people should be responsible to someone else to help them take the necessary procedural steps at the right time.

The group that sets and pursues its goals carefully will discover at the end of the year that most of the goals have been met.

Some will have been accomplished much earlier than everyone ever thought possible. Some goals will have been met only partially, and others will not have been met at all. That's okay. Do not be discouraged if all of your goals are not met every year. Some goals may appear on your list for several years before they are met or abandoned. One of my five-year goals was to establish a Christian elementary school in our community. In nine months after that goal was clarified, I was able to be part of the establishment of a Christian school which included all thirteen grades. That goal was more than met in much less time than I ever dreamed. However, I have had an annual goal of establishing a Christian radio station and a counseling clinic for the past three or four years. Both of these goals are taking much longer to accomplish than I had expected.

As you meet with the leaders of your church, do not always talk about the mechanics of staffing the Sunday school and maintaining the buildings. Spend some time in each session talking about goals. Dr. Donald McGavran has said that a growing church must have both pastor and people who are bold, committed, flexible, and visionary.

Seven
PRACTICE
COURAGE

Amazing! Absolutely amazing! Jesus was in their town and they were asking him to leave. The Gadarenes were frightened by this young rabbi who had just cured the town's biggest problems. Jesus had cast demons out of two men who lived in the local cemetery. Everyone had been frightened of these two wild, raving individuals; and now both of them were calm and sane. Undoubtedly there were other civic problems this prophet could solve also, but the consensus of the population was that he should leave.

Was he really the Messiah, as he claimed, or was he another false prophet? Maybe he was a charlatan. "Perhaps the Romans would not want him to be here. Things *are* pretty peaceful, even under the Roman rule. This miracle worker might upset our political and economic system." The real truth was evident: The people lacked the courage to wrestle with the responsibility that would be theirs if Jesus of Nazareth really *was* God's Son (Matthew 8:28-34).

Unfortunately, many Christians react similarly to their own culture. When new forms are introduced they immediately reject the fad or fashion. Usually the rejection is made on some kind of trumped-up spiritual cause, and, conversely, old forms in the culture are usually accepted without being carefully evaluated. Most Christians, for instance, have accepted the American dream. They continue to push their own standard of living higher and higher. They use (waste?) their time in just about the same way as their unsaved neighbors do. They are as involved in trite conversation, love of athletics, and recreation as the unbeliever with whom they rub elbows each day.

Most Christians have not carefully evaluated their own society. Dr. Francis Schaeffer says, in his movie on the Renaissance (the third movie in the series, "How Should We Then Live?") that Michelangelo's masterpiece "David" is not the biblical David. The well-known sculpture shows the genius of the great Michelangelo. Very few people have seriously studied the master sculptor well enough to make the startling claim that Schaeffer verbalizes His point is that no one was ever as perfect as "David."

It is time for American evangelicals to recognize that the god of America is not the God of the Bible. It is a tragedy that we trust our culture more than we trust our God. We believe the United States Constitution is the document that will protect us and supply us with our rights. Christians have not adequately scrutinized their own government, history, and culture in light of the Scriptures.

It takes a courageous Christian to declare that long hair and a beard on a man are not necessarily a sign of rebellion or an anti-Christian bias. Someone needs to challenge the majority of churchgoers who use Romans 13 as a proof-text to teach us to obey our government regardless of its dictates. "My country, right or wrong" is definitely an anti-Christian concept. Scriptures like 1 Corinthians 6 teach us that government is not capable of settling disputes between Christians. Government should not be so easily and implicitly trusted in other areas either.

Some young, avant-garde Christians today challenge the lifestyle and materialism of older Christians. Yet when I see this happening, I always take a good look at the opposer. Frequently I notice a young college student who is standing in sixty dollars' worth of hiking boots. His body is draped with a down-filled parka worth another $100. It is pure hypocrisy for younger Christians to attack older Christians for their materialism when the attacker simply absorbs and enjoys the materialism of his own parents. It is quite amusing to me to see some of these doing the most talking while they enjoy Daddy's payment of their college or university tuition. Since they do not have to work, they have a great deal of time to attack more conventional Christianity.

To achieve change within the church, we need courageous Christians to serve as catalysts. The believer who devours *Moody Monthly* should also occasionally read *Sojourners* and *The Wittenburg Door*. And those who insist that Christianity is political and economic should force themselves to read *Moody Monthly* and cooperate with the church. The courageous Christian will be willing to stand between the two extremes and challenge both to listen to the other side of evangelicalism and exercise a willingness to be flexible. Certainly it's easier to stand with one biased group and join in carping about the other side; it's more comfortable to stay as we are and not face the challenge from fellow Christians who believe somewhat differently from the way that we interpret the Bible. Some even wanted Jesus to go away from their city so they would not have to face the issues that would confront them.

Courage may help other people to join in the battle. Elijah Lovejoy was a Presbyterian pastor before the Civil War. After observing one lynching, Lovejoy committed himself forever to fighting the awful sin of slavery. Mob action was brought against him time after time. Neither that action nor the many other threats and attempts on his life deterred him. In addition to preaching, he printed a newspaper which attacked the social evil of slavery. Repeated destruction of his presses did not stop him. Once he wrote, "If by compromise is meant that I should cease from my duty, I cannot make it. I fear God more than I fear man. Crush me if you will, but I will die at my post . . ." And die he did, four days later, at the hands of another mob. Not one of the ruffians was prosecuted or indicted or punished in any way for his murder. But the story includes a glad note. One young man was deeply moved by the Lovejoy martyrdom. He had just been elected to the Illinois legislature. His name was Abraham Lincoln.[29]

At a conference a few years ago a young bearded man approached me and asked if I recognized him. I confessed that I did not. He told me that he had attended the small denominational college where I went to school. He was a year or two behind me in the process of education. He left that school in favor of a more broadly based approach to life and ministry. During those days I led several campaigns that were very antitraditional. This fellow wanted me to know that my crusades in college were a great inspiration to him. It was a warm feeling to know that some small amount of courage that I had displayed years earlier had been helpful to another brother. That man has since become a very successful pastor in the Los Angeles area.

Another man who is now a missionary in France had completely given up on the church. He was committed to Jesus Christ, but he had decided that the church had nothing to offer him. He heard of a certain approach which seemed to be different from the traditional churches with which he was acquainted. He tried that church and was impressed. As God continued to work in his life, he soon separated from the Air Force and spent the next four years in seminary. Now he serves the Lord in France. The changes he saw taking place in that church influenced him to join in the effort to create change in other churches around the world.

Only last Sunday after our evening service a young man stayed and talked for some time. His parents are both well-known evangelical leaders in our community. He has not been attending church. I can well imagine that his parents have prayed and wept for him on many occasions. He had avoided attending our church because he supposed it was a traditional church that would not meet his needs. However, after attending two services he was impressed that the church (at least in some cases) may be worth fighting for. He has a renewed interest in the things of God. One church's courage to change may help this young man return to a place of meaningful worship and service of our Lord.

Courage has always been useful to win life's battles. Andrew Jackson said, "One man with courage makes a majority." And when Sir Andrew Browne Cunningham was cornered by the Italian fleet in November 1940, he courageously challenged his own forces with, "We are so outnumbered there is only one thing we can do—we must attack." Chrysostom, threatened by Empress Eudoxia, said, "Go tell her I fear nothing but sin." God has always used people with courage. Moses faced an angry mob at the Red Sea, and on many other occasions, but he accomplished wonders because he courageously stood, realizing that he was a majority with God on his side.

Businessmen have long seen the advantage of courage. It is evident that business growth is not accomplished overnight by blatant advertisements or *blitzkrieg* selling. It is a painstaking process demanding constant courage. There are few shortcuts, but a world of planning, study, and thought. Fate seldom sides with the person who is not equipped with courage. But when the firm has at its top a person with a definite forward policy qualified to think and plan, that firm can exploit its opportunities.

It has been sad to watch men with great gifts and potential fail in ministry. Sometimes that failure is due directly to the lack of courage to try new, innovative, creative methods in the church. The leader who relies on the past and refuses to climb out on a limb will wallow in mediocrity. "The ability to change requires prophetic discernment, self-understanding, and raw courage born of faith."[30]

One of the lessons leaders need to be constantly reminded of is that part of their responsibility is to take the flak. If a leader is not willing to accept criticism, he needs to get out of the position of leadership. Leaders will always be placed in positions that make them vulnerable to one side or the other. Choices must be made. Not everyone will be happy all of the time. Sometimes I wonder if everyone will be happy any of the time.

When the leaders of one particular church wanted to responsibly put before the congregation the options that would help reduce the financial deficit, they were disappointed in some of the responses. The leaders created a survey that asked the people of the church their opinion on what to do with the financial crisis at hand. Up to that point, the leaders had been extremely conservative in managing the church budget. They had sheared the fat and trimmed the bones, and yet remained actively involved in outreach and ministry. In spite of this, some of the respondents to the survey chided the leaders for not being responsible in their handling of the finances.

Since the survey was anonymous, many people took the opportunity to vent their spleens on the leaders for not handling the finances in a more skillful manner. The truth of the matter was that many of the church people who had voted for certain expenditures were not giving proportionately or according to biblical principles that would cover those expenditures by normal offerings. Nevertheless, leaders cannot allow themselves to be discouraged by criticism.

"I can't make that decision now—I'll have to pray about it." With that cliché, many Christians hide the indecision of their own souls. Afraid to make decisions, they let a popular euphemism take the place of decisiveness. In *The Time Trap*, MacKenzie says:

There is a myth that delay improves the quality of decisions. Flory, from the experience of many years as a consultant to executives, says that 15 .. of the problems coming to an executive need to mature, 5 .. shouldn't be answered at all, and the remaining 80 .. should be decided now.[31]

It is true that some Christians simply refuse to make decisions when they need to be made. A medical doctor friend of mine claims to have created his own rule, which bears his name. He informed me that other physicians now refer to this as his own rule. It is that, if he catches himself spending more than five minutes complaining about an employee, then that person should be dismissed from his position. His experience has been that if he must complain about the performance of an employee, then probably that employee cannot be redeemed for his organization. Through the years he has discovered that, as much as he may try another course of action, he still ends up dismissing the person. It never seems to work out to counsel and keep the individual.

That kind of rule is probably too harsh for the body of Christ. Certainly we *can* counsel and redeem people for future useful ministry. Yet there are times when courage to dismiss someone from a certain volunteer or staff position would be the kindest and most efficient way to run the church. It takes courage to confront and dismiss, but surely the church would be operating more effectively if this kind of confrontation occurred. It would certainly make the church business seem more serious to those both inside and outside the institution.

Peter Drucker puts it like this:

Courage rather than analysis dictates the truly important rules for identifying priorities:

1. Pick the future as against the past.
2. Focus on opportunity rather than on a problem.

3. Choose your own direction rather than climb on the band-wagon.
4. Aim high. Aim for something that will make a difference rather than for something that is safe and easy to do.[32]

One of the hardest confrontations any church can endure is to challenge the effectiveness of one of its own missionaries, schools, or denominational agencies. Yet this kind of hard analysis must transpire if we are going to do God's work in a fashion that truly honors him. It seems almost impossible for some churches to muster the courage to dismiss some of their long-time missionaries. This distasteful task must be handled in a proper way that will make missionaries and mission agencies and denominational boards responsible for their actions to the churches.

When one church went through the painful process of evaluating one of its missionaries, it discovered that indeed the denominational headquarters had been dissatisfied with him for some time. The shame of the matter was that they continued to allow the missionary couple to serve in Africa although they were not operating in a manner that pleased anyone or got results for the Lord. The mission agency was confronted with whether or not they were doing anything to help this missionary correct his personal and ministry problems. They were not. The church then decided that it had an obligation to no longer support that couple. It was a hard decision, but they have never been sorry for taking that courageous step.

On another occasion a church discovered that one of its missionaries held several beliefs significantly different from their own. That missionary happened to be from their own denomination and worked in their own city on a college campus. He had been quite successful in evangelism, and many of the college students were currently attending the sponsoring church. The church leaders tried to act responsibly in the matter. They appointed a three-man ad hoc committee to interview the campus worker to discover if the charges were true. The investigation showed that the missionary would soon be leaving the city and moving on to another ministry. It would have been easy for the church to simply not face the doctrinal issues—to drop the matter and not cause waves. This would allow them to have a nice going-away affair for the missionary and say kind words about him. They *were* certainly pleased with the way God had used him in their city. But the doctrinal issues were in areas of major importance to the church. As the leaders discussed the matter they felt they must take a more difficult and courageous path and finish their investigation. They did, and they committed themselves to bringing the confrontation before the whole church body. The confrontation brought some ugly results, yet, the leaders are sure they made the right choice.

I have known other churches that support missionaries, denominations, and institutions who are not doing a good job for God. Some even support people they wholeheartedly disagree with. Some support individuals who are lazy and sloppy in the ministry. Yet for lack of courage they continue their support. Surely God is not pleased with such lack of courage.

Those who wish to create change in the church must work to keep the church pure before God. When there is open and blatant sin in the congregation, it must be confronted according to the principles of Matthew 18. On more than just a few occasions I have known church leaders who have gone into homes and confronted sin that affects the church and the community. Sometimes these leaders have suffered abuse, shoutings, and cursings. Yet they continue to act in a manner that forces the congregation to believe that the Bible must be taken seriously when it calls believers to live a holy and righteous life.

Those wishing to effect change in the church must be careful not to lead crusades for the sake of their own egos. They must constantly beware of putting themselves into the spotlight for the sake of applause. Yet the church leader who displays courage will find those who are willing to follow. He will inspire others that the Bible is serious concerning the place of the church in the world today.

Eight
PROTECT
PEOPLE

Effective leadership is an art and a science. It is an art because it involves God-given, innate abilities. It is a science because it involves learned skills.

The art of leadership deals with what you are. In Numbers 16 Moses shows us part of what a leader is. A leader is a person of compassion. In that chapter Moses was having a confrontation with Korah. God warned Korah through Moses that he should not oppose his chosen leader. But Korah continued to oppose Moses. So God opened up the earth and swallowed up the complainers. Then God sent fire from heaven and more were killed. The next day, according to verse 41, the people came and complained against Moses and said that he had killed the people. God said to Moses, "Move over. I'll finish the job." But Moses fell on his face and asked God not to kill the people. Moses was a man of compassion. That's part of what a leader must be. One experienced administrator puts it like this: "Leadership is not something you *do*; it is something you *are*."[33]

Henry and Ann, both in their early thirties, were having marital problems. They were struggling to discover themselves and one another in their marriage. The result was a separation. But they were well established in the church and had been serving the Lord faithfully for years. That was the problem. The difficulty in this separation was that Henry and Ann were the young people's directors in their church. They taught the high school group. Soon the teen-agers knew something was wrong, and discovered the difficulty. Ann had left Henry. In fact she was having a relationship with another man in the church. No one believed that the relationship was sexual, but she admitted that she was struggling to decide between the other man and her own husband of eight years. As parents of the teen-agers learned of the difficulty, they began complaining to the leaders of the church that Henry should resign his position. "It's bad enough to have any Christian couple separate, but when they are the young people's directors, it sets a bad example for the teen-agers," said the parents.

Undoubtedly the parents were right. It was a bad example. Yet the leaders of the church kindly expressed to each of the complaining parents that almost all marriages have bumpy places from time to time. Henry and Ann were no different. It was true that they had a different place of responsibility, and they were running the risk of damaging young, fragile lives. Nonetheless the church leaders stood firm in their support of Henry's continuing in the young people's ministry. And as the leaders worked and prayed to see Henry and Ann reconciled, they were willing to take the criticism of many parents (and, in fact, some nonparents), because the couple had done such a wonderful job ministering to the teen-agers and the kids had responded warmly to them.

The end result of this particular situation was that Ann returned home to her husband. Their marriage is now stronger than ever. The teen-agers who knew of the difficulty have renewed admiration for the church. The church did not dump the young people's directors simply because they were having a marital difficulty. The church does not expect perfection. It is not a place for those who have no problems. The church is a place for those who have problems but are willing to work on them. Henry had agreed that if the problem continued much longer, he would resign. Both he and his wife were grateful for the support of the church leaders through that crisis in their lives.

The Mountain View Church has a different kind of problem. One of the fine, godly men of that church has a wife with severe emotional and mental disturbances. This woman has a compulsion to serve the Lord. Her motives seemed pure at first, but it is now evident that her compulsion is a result of her neurosis. She is emotionally unstable, extremely nervous, and has difficulty relating to any person. Her behavior is erratic, and she has caused many difficulties through the years when the leaders at Mountain View have tried to give her places of responsibility. Psychiatrists, psychologists, and Christian counselors have not been able to discover the root of her problem and give her the assistance she needs in order to find rest in Christ.

So the leaders of Mountain View have decided that Mrs. Bradbury cannot serve in their particular setting. They have not yet been able to discover any job or ministry that she could handle. Each time they've tried, the result has been disastrous. Even working alone has not yet been successful. Rather than exposing this woman or being unkind, they have agreed to simply be vague. At first they tried the method of loving confrontation, but Mrs. Bradbury could not understand the approach. She would quickly forget what was said and return to the same harangue. So now the leaders simply let her criticize and complain about having no place of ministry. Several of the leaders of the church are confronted weekly by the woman as she volunteers for more and more places of ministry. During the past few years she has volunteered for almost every job in the church. When a vague answer is given, she seems satisfied, but will return the next week to ask for another job.

The truth is that the work of the church is to protect people. People are more important than institutions. People are more important than perfection at all levels of life. People are more important than the organization. People are more important than the smooth operation of the group. Furthermore, people are not statistics. How discouraging it is to hear the newscaster drone on the radio: "Another fatality on Interstate 40 today, which brings the total for the year to 356 dead. That compares with 359 killed in highway accidents by this date last year."

Jim was teaching his class in the Sunday school adult elective program. During one class period he mentioned the high rate of venereal disease in the city where he lived. "In fact," he said, "one out of every ten people in this city has V.D. When you pass ten people on the street, one of them has a venereal disease." Then he addressed a city policeman who was a member of the class. He remarked that he probably would have much more information on the subject. But the policeman did not respond. He called his name a second time, and there was no response. Obviously he was preoccupied with another matter. When Jim called the officer's name the third time and asked what he was doing, the policeman responded, "I'm counting out ten people." The truth is, you cannot just count people and learn anything about them. The church has often been guilty of running over the very people that it has been trying to minister to.

In 1933 Dr. Albert Einstein visited his friend, Beno Gutenberg, the distinguished professor of seismology at Cal Tech. The two thinkers strolled around the campus, wholly absorbed in a conversation about earthquakes. Suddenly they became aware of people rushing from buildings around them. Then they realized that the earth was quaking under their feet. "We had become so involved in seismology," Gutenberg recalled later, "that we hadn't noticed the biggest earthquake I'd ever experienced—taking place right under us." The same kind of experience can easily happen to church members. Sometimes they get so involved with the work of the ministry that they forget people. Engrossed in the mechanics of the church, leaders overlook the very people God has called them to minister to.

Before Brownstreet Church moved its primaries from one room and put the juniors into that room, they did not talk with the teachers of either department. The Sunday school super-intendent thought the change was needed because of the larger number of juniors who needed the more spacious room. Yet in his desire to perform his duty, he had overlooked the important principle of this chapter. Sometimes even those who are involved in specialized ministries to the retarded or deaf or other handi-capped people discover that they have served with such exu-berance that they have, in fact, overlooked the individual person-alities and needs of their own students.

As a hospital chaplain I saw that it was possible for those in that type of ministry to become so accustomed to suffering and pain that, in fact, they overlooked what was going on around them. They saw people as patients but not as people. They became hardened to the misery with which they dealt every day. It sur-prises some people to discover that ministers often rate very low in compassion. Some psychologists theorize that this is the way the minister protects himself from the pain that he sees every day. Certainly it is true that, if the doctor or minister or counselor became emotionally involved in every situation, he would "bleed to death" before he could make it to the safety of his home in the evening. It is true that the mind and heart are limited as to the burdens they can bear, but nonetheless Christians must always be careful not to get so heavily involved in running the program and making the changes that they forget to empathize with people.

"Does anyone have a church list? Let's go through the list and see whom we can get to teach the junior high class." That approach, unfortunately, is often the one a Christian education committee takes when it gets together to "fill the slot" that was left vacant by a resignation. How much more profitable it would be if churches would carefully and prayerfully search out the people of God's choosing for every position in the church. At first it might seem to take longer to develop such an approach. Yet the long-term result will be that those ministering in each place will be the ones chosen and called by God. Furthermore, the more prayerful method of recruiting is a safeguard against overloading willing workers with too many responsibilities in the church. The wise church leader will be cautious not to place too many responsibilities upon the shoulders of those who are willing to get involved.

When Pastor Bruce accepted his new responsibilities at Lakeside Community Church, he immediately wanted to change the carpet in the church office. He was quite adamant about "that ugly blue carpet." Little did he know that Mrs. Griffin had given that carpet as a memorial to her late husband. Immediately the new pastor was in disfavor with one of the power people in the church. His proposed change had rolled right over a body. In another church the board of elders wanted to change the teacher in the "Win One Class" (the class for senior citizens). Little did they realize that they were in for the fight of their lives. Mr. Francis had taught that class for the past decade. He was willing to move to another position, but the class was not about to give him up so easily. The elders had to weigh the advantage of making the change against the trauma they were going to cause among the class members and, in fact, throughout the whole church.

Bob, an insurance salesman, was a member of his church's

board of deacons. When the church started talking about the need for a new accounting system, he was interested. He had read a few books on the subject and was personally challenged by various methods of accounting. He immediately volunteered to take on the project and change the books to a system he had developed. The problem was that the other men on the board did not think he was qualified. He was offended. He felt that his system was superior to any system the deacons might obtain from an accountant. The other board members did not want to further offend Bob, but they did not feel that they could allow his system to be instituted as the official church accounting system. After delicate conversation week after week in board meetings, the group finally decided that an outside firm would be hired to put the church on a standard accounting system. Bob got a certain amount of satisfaction since some of his ideas were incorporated into the system proposed by the professional accountant. An individual's ego had been bent but not broken, and the church leaders had made a responsible decision.

When one tries to protect people rather than an organization, there is a natural tension in many churches. Most Christians believe that there are absolutes which dictate even over the feelings of any individual. For instance, when there is sin in the church the Bible does teach (Matthew 18) that the sin should be removed from the congregation. One church discovered that a former adult Sunday school teacher and church leader was having an affair with a secretary at his place of employment. When the matter was discovered, he moved to another state. His family was to follow later. He and his wife reconciled their differences through the painful experience. The church decided that to publicly discipline the man would actually serve no value. He was already located in a different place, and the only ones to suffer would be his family.

That same church faced another situation when two of its single adult members were living together as though they were married. The church sent several delegations to counsel and talk with the offenders. Love was expressed, and concern was voiced.

Nevertheless, the two would neither marry nor discontinue the practice of living together. The church therefore did bring their names and the facts to a public meeting. They were exposed and dismissed from the church membership. There *are* times when doctrinal purity must prevail over the rights and privileges of any individual or group. Each situation must be carefully evaluated on its own merits.

Roy had been a deacon in his church for the past thirty-five years. Now he was somewhat senile, but every three years the congregation continued to elect him to the board. As new men came into the leadership of the church, they began to question the wisdom of having someone on the board who was not functioning properly as a leader of the body. Yet those who had been members of the church for decades believed that it was not harmful to allow Roy to stay on the board. He really was not cantankerous, and he did not cause any particular problem. In fact, he was unable to attend many of the board meetings. The church leaders had to decide at this point whether or not to keep Roy and protect a person or do that which was more expedient for the entire church. Those decisions are always difficult to make, and they will be made properly only through honest discussion and prayer to understand the mind of the Lord in each individual situation.

Mr. Witherspoon had been a member of his church for twenty-two years when a new pastor arrived. For the last eight years he had proudly held the position of head usher. The new pastor related warmly to Mr. Witherspoon. As head usher, Witherspoon did all he could to help the pastor during the morning and evening worship services. Soon, however, as the church began to grow, it was evident that the head usher needed to select and train additional people to help with the duties that were now being demanded. No longer was it only a responsibility to distribute bulletins and pass the offering plate once per service. Now the head usher had to direct the setting up of chairs. Furthermore, the leaders of the church decided that people should be ushered to seats rather than allowed to find their own seats in the auditorium. Then the church went to two services on Sunday morning because of the crowded conditions. Now twice as many ushers needed to be recruited and trained. This whole affair was clearly getting out of the hands of Mr. Witherspoon. He no longer wanted to give the amount of time and attention to the job that it was beginning to require. So at the next annual meeting he declined the nomination as head usher.

It was only a year later that Gary Peters quit his job as treasurer of the same church. For years he had proudly held that position, but as the church grew, the position became much more complicated and detailed. Like Mr. Witherspoon, his best friend, he had clearly gotten in over his head at this point. Neither man was willing to accept additional responsibilities, and neither was willing to pursue further training to help prepare them for their places of ministry. The point is that as change does occur, some people will probably be left wounded and lying in the dust. Some of those bodies are there because of their own choices. The wise and godly leader will try to prevent personal devastation as much as possible, but again he should realize that certain conditions may occur which will mean less than perfect relationships with some of the new and former members of the church.

The leader who wishes to create orderly change within the church will be a person of compassion and kindness. He will not always put efficiency and the organization before people. He will see people as individuals and not as statistics. He will not try to push people into slots, but will rather learn who people are so that he can help create ministries for them. In effecting any change in the church, he will try to discover the background of the context so that he will not be offensive in creating change in that particular situation. Nonetheless, he will realize that there are times when people do get hurt. His primary principle still remains: Protect people.

Nine
PREACH
GRACE

Preachers are people too. Often someone will approach me after a service and say, "Pastor, that message really worked on my life." My response is, "It worked on mine too." Part of the dynamic of preaching is that the preacher first deals with the passage as it touches his own life. Only after the Scripture has spoken to me can I speak with authority to others. And since preachers are people too, it must be true that passages apply with varying degrees of pressure and comfort to the preacher.

The truth of this chapter is one that has dramatically touched my life. This truth has been working on me for years. Although I was raised in a system that does not really understand or teach this truth, I knew it was there. When I have had opportunity I have spoken about this subject. Sometimes I have been branded a maverick or radical by those who disagree. Several events and studies have combined to teach me this truth in a new way in recent years. I will never be the same. I write this chapter from the very depths of my heart.

The relevance of this truth can be shown by asking one simple question: Is God pleased with you? Answer that before reading the next sentence. "Is God pleased with you?" If you answer *no* or if you hesitate to answer yes, then you need this truth as badly as I do, or maybe even more than I do.

Most of us were either raised in or exposed to a fundamentalism or evangelicalism that has taught us to be negative. We emphasize man's sinfulness. We try to motivate ourselves and others through guilt. Have you ever noticed how much of our evangelical preaching is negative? Even when we preach on joy our emphasis is, "You are not joyful enough." When we preach about love we conclude, "None of us loves enough." We try to get Christians in gear by making them feel guilty. This is the way to try to motivate people to change.

But the New Testament does not do that. The message of that book is called *gospel*—good news. The good news is that as Christians, God is pleased with us. Did you read that correctly? Read it again. That is good news—God is pleased with you.

Ephesians 1 surely teaches that. God has blessed us with every spiritual blessing (v. 3). He has chosen us (v. 4). We are holy and blameless (v. 4). We are the praise of his glory (vv. 6, 12, 14), or the displays of his grace. As you read that chapter you cannot find one thing any of us did to deserve any of the blessings listed. It is all by grace.

Now answer these questions: How were you saved—by works or by grace? How are you trying to grow in your Christian life—by works or by grace? Are you trying to earn God's favor by works?

Paul put it this way in Galatians 3:3: "Then have you gone completely crazy? For if trying to obey the Jewish laws never gave you spiritual life in the first place, why do you think that trying to obey them now will make you stronger Christians?" (*The Living Bible*). The point is simple: We must not attempt to earn our salvation; we need only accept it. And as Christians, too, we must not try to earn God's favor. We need only accept it. We must learn to accept God's grace. That's what Ephesians 2:8-10 says.

God's grace is free. "For it is by grace you have been saved, through faith—and this not of yourself; it is the gift of God—not of works so that no one can boast" (Ephesians 2:8,9).

The nature of grace is that it doesn't cost anything. Aristotle defined grace as "that which is bestowed freely with no expectations of return. It is an act which finds its only motive in the goodheartedness of the giver." Theologically the word is usually defined as "everything for nothing for those who deserve the worst." It is a gift with no strings attached.

In our society we teach the Puritan work ethic of paying our way and working for what we get. Therefore it is a shock to really understand free grace. Actually it is redundant to speak of "free" grace. Romans 11:6 shows that grace isn't really grace if it is involved with works at all. Works and grace are mutually exclusive. One who thinks he merits heaven has no understanding of God's holiness or of his own sinfulness. Ephesians 2:1-3 explains that we were dead without God. We could not respond to him. Isaiah 64:6 says even our so-called "righteousness" is as filthy rags before God.

In ancient times a lawmaker, Zuculous, declared that anyone

caught in adultery would have both of his eyes gouged out. The first guilty person brought before the lawmaker was his own son. He decreed that he was guilty, and he sentenced his son to have one of his eyes punched out. Zuculous then had one of his own eyes punched out to meet the demands of the law. In more modern times I read of a man who stole some milk from a grocery store. Broke and out of a job, he stole to feed his family. The judge declared him guilty and sentenced him to pay a $10 fine. Since he had no money, the man naturally thought he would go to jail to serve out the fine. But the judge suddenly stepped from the bench, reached into his own wallet and paid the $10. Then from his own wallet he gave the man an extra $10. The man was guilty and had to be judged such, but the one who judged him was also the one who paid the penalty. That is what Jesus has done for us.

Grace is difficult to accept. It is our natural tendency to boast. Pride keeps many from receiving Christ. Some fear what others will think. Some fear the humble act of baptism after salvation. Pride prevents some Christians from experiencing God's grace. Most of us in the helping professions have a touch of the "Messiah complex." (See chapter 2.) The attitude is noble, but it sets us up for doing things our own way instead of depending upon God's grace. It is true that hard work and lots of love will solve many problems. But once one gets into that syndrome it becomes difficult to relax and let God run matters. Pride of accomplishment is the opposite of accepting God's grace. This is an important lesson for the leader who wants to create change in the church. Self-satisfaction can be dangerous. It is an offense to God, and it hinders Christians in their growth.

One who deems himself unworthy to receive God's grace may have big problems which prevent him from coming to God for full blessing. One who can't accept God's forgiveness will find it difficult to forgive others. One who can't accept God's grace will not find it easy to be gracious and kind to others. This type of individual is always working to meet his own standards. He drives himself, his family, and his colleagues too hard. He and everyone around him are pressured and unhappy. He may try to fool himself into thinking his hard work is motivated purely by a desire to change things for the better. He may even piously proclaim that his drive for excellence is to please God. But down deep the problem is that he hasn't accepted God's grace. He always feels guilty. He is always working to get God's favor rather than simply receiving God's grace.

It isn't easy to give up and let God run your life. Everything in us resists that move. It is natural to want to do it ourselves, to work for our rewards. But salvation and the Christian life are free. Both come from grace. So relax and accept what God has already done. Let God guide you in accepting compromises, in setting goals, in organizing, in establishing priorities.

"This," says Ephesians 2:8, "is the gift of God." Some believe grace is the gift of God spoken of here. Obviously, but that is not what the verse teaches. (It is the wrong gender in the original Greek.) Others believe faith is the gift of God, but in the Greek the word *faith* is also in the wrong gender. Both grace and faith are feminine while "this" is neuter. The Apostle Paul is saying that the whole process is the gift of God. It is wrong to say that grace is God's part and faith is ours. Even human relationships teach that our faith in one another is based upon what that individual has shown himself to be. Faith may be defined as "an active response built upon an attitude of confidence, based upon what the other person reveals himself to be." That definition forces us to trust the Lord for the changes he wants in his church.

Salvation is by grace alone. This is true because God is perfect. No works are acceptable for the payment of sin. Ephesians 2:9 is plain: not of works. How do you interpret that verse? Salvation is a gift from God because we have not only sinned against God's law, but also against his love. Suppose that a man negligently runs over a child with his car. He then serves three years in prison for that criminal act. When he is released from prison the law has no more demand upon him. Yet, if he is to be forgiven by the mother of the child, it will be because she decides to forgive. He has sinned not only against the law but against love. So only love can forgive. That is why we can never earn our salvation. If we are to be forgiven, it will be because God has decided to forgive us.

During World War 2 Frank Gajowniczek, a sergeant in the Polish Army, was captured by the Nazis and sent to a prison camp in Germany. One day in July 1941 some prisoners escaped. As a retaliatory move the Nazis arbitrarily selected ten other prisoners to die of starvation. Gajowniczek was one of the ten. He complained that he did not want to die because he wanted to return to his wife and family again. Then a Franciscan monk, Maximillian Kolbe, stood up and asked if he could take the sergeant's place. The monk was allowed to do so, and he starved to death with the other nine men. Now each year Gajowniczek places a wreath on Kolbe's grave to remind him of the man who died in his place. Jesus died in your place, not just so you could live another few years on this planet, but so you could live forever. But only those who have accepted God's grace will be allowed into God's heaven.

God's grace can solve your problems, even the problems of provincialism in your church. The Greek idea of grace was kindness to a friend. The Greeks never thought of grace given to an enemy. That is where God's grace is different. While we were still God's enemies he supplied grace for all our needs. Our responsibility now is to accept God's grace. We don't have to earn it to be saved. We don't have to earn it to get his blessing on our lives or on our churches. God is happy with you. Accept his grace. As L. Nelson Bell once wrote, "One of the signs of spiritual maturity is a growing realization of the grace of God."

Norm Van Brocklin, while coach of the Minnesota Vikings, let his players know that he would not pull them from the game because they made a mistake. He believed that having people work under that kind of pressure was harmful to the man and to his performance, as well as to the entire team. He let all of the players know that their performance was not the condition for his blessing.

Now as Christians we should not live under the pressure of trying to make God happy with us. He is already happy with us.

Isn't that wonderful? Doesn't that cause a sigh of relief? *That* is good news! When Christians hear this message they are more inclined to try creative change. They no longer must "play it safe" with God for fear of offending him. Change comes easier to the one who understands grace.

A few years ago a prominent religious man of the United States died. A U.S. Senator eulogized him and said, "He will never have to account for his stewardship, for if his goodness is not known to God, no one's ever will be." But God is not looking for our goodness. It is a common mistake among mortals to believe that salvation comes by works, but the Bible plainly refutes that. The other half of grace is often missed too. Christians work, work, work to try to please God rather than simply learning to accept God's grace for daily living. I don't know how else to say it—God's grace is free.

God's grace creates a response (Ephesians 2:10). Grace produces help in the Christian life. It produces power (2 Corinthians 12:9) and godly living (Titus 2:11,12). Grace also teaches the truth (2 Peter 3:17,18) and helps in time of need (Hebrews 4:16). Furthermore, grace opens up opportunities for evangelism (Colossians 4:6) and endures unjust suffering (1 Peter 2:19). And grace spreads among Christians as a sweet aroma to God (2 Corinthians 2:14,15).

There is something else grace does—it produces good works, according to Ephesians 2:10. The Bible does not speak against good works—it only warns that we are not to trust good works for salvation or for blessing.

We are God's workmanship. The Greek word translated "workmanship" is used only here and in Romans 1:20, which speaks of what God has made. The Greek word means the product of an action. It is the word from which we get our English word "poem." The imagery is that we have been put together by God as a poet puts together words to create a beautiful lyric.

We are created unto good works, according to this verse. There is a parallelism here with Genesis 1. In the beginning God's Spirit moved and created something out of nothing. Now God's Spirit moves and creates spiritual life out of spiritually dead people. That produces beautiful change in his church.

The Greek does not say that we are created in Christ *in order that* we might perform good works. God did not save us so we could serve him. That would mean his purpose was to get something from us—and that wouldn't be grace. But salvation now gives us the potential and possibility of good works we couldn't do before salvation.

The works are good from God's point of view, not man's. We must remember to define good works as God does. Sometimes the world system will not think a good work really is good. And other times the world system will want us to do things that they call good but God calls rotten.

Our good works have already been prepared for us, says the last phrase of Ephesians 2:10. Long before we were born, the good works were prepared in God's sovereignty. We didn't even have any part in thinking up the good works. Our response is now that God has given so much grace, we can't wait to serve him. Now we just live by grace and discover the works he has prepared. We don't create the good works; we simply discover the ones he has already prepared for us and for his church.

Isn't it marvelous? God's grace has supplied it all. If you really grasp this truth, it should change you. Don't feel guilty anymore. Don't go to church or Bible studies because you feel you must. Serve God with gladness, not as a burden.

Is God pleased with you? Yes, he is, if you are a believer. Now live with that in mind. Accept God's grace for salvation *and for Christian living*. Live with that acceptance. Enjoy it. Freely set about to change the church in an orderly way. But always remember who the church belongs to. Don't get frustrated at what seems to be a lack of progress. Soak up the grace in every situation. Exhort others to understand God's grace so that they too will learn to relax and help the church to change—to do a better job for Jesus.

APPENDIX A

Evaluation of the Ministries at Temple

Please help evaluate Temple's ministries by putting a check where appropriate.

Ministry	Strength	Need Change	New Emphasis
Sunday A.M. Service			
Sunday P.M. Service			
Music			
Ushers			
Communion			
Baptism			
Flowers			
Tape			
Greeters			
Sunday School			
Pioneer Girls			
Boys Brigade			
Choirs			
Camping Program			
Bookstore			
Library/Audiovisual			
Singles			
Nursery			
Children's Church			
Visitation			
Home, Wednesday Bible Studies			

Ministry	Strength	Need Change	New Emphasis
Coffee House			
Evangelistic Dinners			
Young People's Activities			
Missions			
Tracts			
Elders Groups			
Supportive Groups			
Sports			
Widows			
Sick			
Hospitality			
Records			
Publications			
Office Work			
Publicity			
Blood Bank			
Finances			
Purchases			
Building Coordination			
Maintenance & Cleaning			
New Buildings			

(This form was first mailed to each member with a cover letter explaining that the member should complete the form. Within two weeks he will receive a phone call from an interviewer to set up an appointment. Then the interviewer will come to his home and talk about this form and ask additional questions.)

Interview

Purpose:

1. To allow the members to evaluate the programs, procedures, and ministries of Temple so as to maintain those features that are functioning properly, and to adjust those that are not.

2. To help the body grow, and the outreach increase, through maintaining or adjusting ourselves to *your* observations.

3. To see where you as a member of the church fit in or could fit in to some areas of #1 Purpose or #2 Purpose.

Take three of the "strength" items checked. Ask, "What makes it a strength?"

\# _____ a.

\# _____ b.

\# _____ c.

Take three of the "need change" items checked and ask, "What is the change you suggest? Why?"

\# _____ a.

\# _____ b.

\# _____ c.

Take three of the "new emphasis" items checked and ask, "Why is this new emphasis or new ministry needed?"

\# _____ a.

\# _____ b.

\# _____ c.

Ask, "What can you do and what are you willing to do based on your evaluation?"

I would like to serve in area(s) \# _____.

In what areas do you need help in your Christian life?

Personal devotions? Family devotions? Bible study? Relating Christ to your marriage? Raising children? Prayer?

(This form was completed by the interviewer as he talked with the member. The member had already completed a form which helped him evaluate every area of ministry of the church.)

Ministry Area: _____

To: _____

We have concluded our survey of the members of the church. For this to be used and for the church to profit from this we need the help and involvement of you as leader of your area of ministry. We received many candid and helpful and even, perhaps, some misinformed comments on your area. We are interested in changing where the change seems needed; continuing where the strength is obvious; and helping inform where the comments are misinformed. To do this you and your help are of crucial importance. You have the complete interview package for your area right here:

a. The total number of comments made about your area

b. The comments themselves broken down into: strengths, suggested changes, and new ministries—new emphases

c. A list of people who voiced an interest in serving in your area for you to use as needed. They have been contacted; they have indicated an interest in your program; and their names are in your hands.

Please look over the comments by section (strengths, changes, new emphasis) and do the following:

1. Pick at least two comments from the strengths that you feel need publicity as a strength, and make the comment below as to which you chose.
2. Pick at least two comments from the changes that you would be willing to consider and that you will incorporate, and make the comment below.
3. Pick two areas of new ministry or new emphasis that you feel are significant and need attention in the future, and make the comment below.
4. Pick two areas from the whole survey where you feel the evaluations are misjudged and misinformed. Where is there a need to make members more aware that this criticism is wrong?

Strengths:	1.
	2.
Changes:	1.
	2.
New Emphasis:	1.
	2.
Misinformed evaluation:	1.
	2.

The Survey

Total Numbers:

Strengths _____ Changes _____
New Emphasis/Ministry _____

List of interested people:

1.
2.
3.
4.
5.
6.
7.
8.
9.
10.
11.
12.
13.
14.
15.

The comments make up the remainder of the survey.

This survey, when completed by you, should be returned to:

Name: _____ Date: _____

(This form was given to each person in charge of a ministry area. All comments about his area were included. He then had to read those comments and complete this form.)

APPENDIX B

Results of Questionnaire

1. Age: 20-40   74%
         40-50   9%
         over 50   7%

2. How long a Christian?
   37% under 5 years
   72% under 10 years

3. Member of Temple?
   52% yes
   48% no

4. How long a member?
   less than 3 years   56%
   less than 5 years   82%
   over 10 years   10%

5. Last year completed in school:
   High school   29%
   College   50%
   Grad. work   21%

6. How long married?
   less than 15 years   30%
   less than 10 years   62%
   less than 20 years   83%
   more than 20 years   17%

7. How many children?
   1-2   61%

8. How long lived in Colorado Springs?
   less than 3 years   31%
   less than 5 years   63%
   less than 10 years   88%

9. Plan to live in Colorado Springs:
   less than 5 years   40%
   more than 5 years   12%
   Indefinitely   14%
   Unsure   41%

10. Politically lean toward:
    liberal   8%
    conservative   64%
    unsure   28%

11. Normally attend Sunday school:
    87% yes
    13% no

12. Do you attend weekly Bible study?
    83% yes
    17% no

13. Regularly maintain private devotions?
    67% yes
    33% no

14. Give at least 10% to God's work?
    65% yes
    35% no

Continuing Goals at Temple

The goal of Temple is to glorify God by cooperating with him as he builds his church. We believe this is best accomplished by providing opportunities for Christians to be involved in evangelism, discipleship, fellowship, and worship.

The emphasis of the church is verse-by-verse Bible teaching. We believe that Christians grow faster and deeper through a clear understanding of God's Word. The primary approach of the church is to help people spiritually by teaching them to understand and practice the principles of the Bible.

This approach works itself out into specific goals in seven areas.

The Goal Is That . . .

Spiritual Growth Goals

1. Each member grow in Christ
   — by spending time daily with God in prayer and Bible study
   — by incorporating scriptural principles into daily life
2. Each family have daily devotions together
3. We learn to worship God individually and corporately

Evangelism Goals

1. Each member be able to share his faith clearly with others
2. Regular witnessing take place in each member's life
3. A steady flow of people come to know Christ personally through the members of Temple
4. A steady flow of people come to know Christ personally through the evangelistic ministries of Temple (college, coffee house, home Bible studies, campground, clubs, men's luncheons, banquets, retreats, camps, etc.)
5. Each family unit serve as a point of evangelism in its own neighborhood

Education Goals

1. All members receive help in discovering their spiritual gifts and using them in meaningful ministries
2. Our Sunday school and clubs continue to teach the Bible in depth and apply its principles to life
3. Temple continue to take a leading role in Christian education for grades K—12
4. Temple continue its education on a formal level through the Colorado Springs Christian Institute
5. Temple continue to support Christian colleges and theological seminaries

Fellowship Goals

1. Each member be related to a small group of people in the church for the purpose of in-depth sharing
2. Each person at Temple be related to a group of people for the purpose of friendship and Christian growth
3. Each person at Temple feel vitally related to the entire church

Community Goals

1. Temple be concerned for the practical, daily needs of people in the community, and provide a means of meeting those needs
2. Concern be expressed for the morality of the community and wherever possible we work for bringing community standards in line with the Bible's directives
3. Temple members take places of responsibility in the community

Music Goals

1. The music ministry of the church assist in worship and praise each Sunday
2. The choirs and special numbers give expressions of the individuals' praise and testimonies
3. We teach biblical truth through music
4. We use music evangelistically
   — at special performances at Temple
   — at banquets and special meetings
5. We provide special musicals several times a year to assist the congregation in worship and praise

Missions Goals

1. Temple take an increasing responsibility in home and foreign missions by giving more prayer and financial support
2. Temple encourage and help its own members to enter vocational missionary service

FOOTNOTES

[1] Howard A. Snyder, *The Problem of Wine Skins*. Downers Grove, Ill.: Inter-Varsity, 1975, p. 15.

[2] Alvin Toffler, *Future Shock*. New York: Random House, 1970, p. 215.

[3] Peter F. Drucker, *The Effective Executive*. New York: Harper & Row, 1966, p. 108.

[4] Lyle E. Schaller, *The Change Agent*. Nashville, Tenn.: Abingdon, 1972, p. 138.

[5] Alan R. Tippett, *Church Growth and the Word of God*. Grand Rapids, Mich.: Eerdmans, 1970, p. 60.

[6] Ray C. Stedman, *Body Life*. Glendale, Calif.: Regal, 1972, p. 16.

[7] Harold Lindsell, *The World, the Flesh, and the Devil*. Washington, D.C.: Canon, 1973, p. 193.

[8] Findley B. Edge, *The Greening of the Church*. Waco, Texas: Word, 1971, p. 20.

[9] Monsma, *The Unraveling of America*. Downers Grove, Ill.: Inter-Varsity, 1974, p. 55.

[10] Alvin Toffler, *Future Shock*. New York: Random House, 1970, p. 187.

[11] Os Guinness, *The Dust of Death*. Downers Grove, Ill.: Inter-Varsity, 1973, p. 23.

[12] Lyle E. Schaller, *The Change Agent*. Nashville, Tenn.: Abingdon, 1972, pp. 58-60.

[13] Robert Townsend, *Up the Organization*. New York: Fawcett World Library, 1971, p. 96.

[14] Albert J. Sullivan, "The Right to Fail," *Journal of Higher Education* (April, 1963), p. 191.

[15] Peter F. Drucker, *The Effective Executive*. New York: Harper & Row, 1966.

[16] R. Alec MacKenzie, *The Time Trap*. New York: McGraw Hill, 1975, p. 53.

[17] *Ibid*, p. 53.

[18] Howard Butt, *Velvet Covered Brick*. New York: Harper & Row, 1973, p. 40.

[19] Willner, *Charismatic Political Leadership*. p. 61.

[20] Robert Townsend, *Up the Organization*. New York: Fawcett World Library, 1971, p. 96.

[21] Rensis Likert and Jane Likert, *New Ways of Managing Conflict*. New York: McGraw Hill, 1976.

[22] *Christian Leadership Letter*, April, 1975, Monrovia, Calif.: World Vision.

[23] Walt Henrichsen, *Disciples Are Made Not Born*. Wheaton, Ill.: Victor, 1974, p. 76.

[24] Edgar Jackson, *Coping with the Crises in Your Life*. New York: Hawthorne, 1974, p. 165.

[25] Ted Engstrom, *The Making of a Christian Leader*. Grand Rapids: Zondervan, 1976, p. 69.

[26] J. D. Batten, *Tough-Minded Management*. American Management Association, 1963, pp. 75,76.

[27] Alec MacKenzie, *Managing Time at the Top*. New York: The Presidents Association, 1970,

[28] Robert Schuller, *Your Church Has Real Responsibilities*. Glendale, Calif.: Regal, 1974, p. 72.

[29] Karl Menninger, *Whatever Became of Sin?* New York: Hawthorn Books, Inc., 1974, p. 210.

[30] Ralph Osborn & Bruce Larson, *The Emerging Church*. Waco, Texas: Word Books, 1970, p. 140.

[31] R. Alec MacKenzie, *The Time Trap*. New York: McGraw Hill, 1975, p. 114.

[32] Peter Drucker, *The Effective Executive*. New York: Harper & Row, 1966, p. 111.

[33] Howard Butt, *The Velvet Covered Brick*. New York: Harper & Row, 1973, p. 36.

DATE DUE